WHEN GOD
GIVES A GIFT

WHEN GOD GIVES A GIFT

In Memoriam of
Layke Huxton Miller
2019 ~ 2020

TAYLOR & CANDACE MILLER

MILLER
BOOKS

MILLER
B O O K S

For information about special discounts for bulk purchases or author interviews, appearances, and speaking engagements please contact:

taylor.miller1515@gmail.com

First Edition

Edited, designed, and produced by Rodney Miles

<u>James 1:17</u>

"Every good gift and every perfect gift is from above, and cometh down from the Father of lights, with whom is no variableness, neither shadow of turning."

King James Version (KJV)
https://www.kingjamesbibleonline.org/James-1-17/

Contents

Introduction

IT WAS A SUNNY Saturday afternoon at the beginning of
November. In Vashti, North Carolina this is a very beautiful
time of year. The leaves change their color and the view
across the mountains is very peaceful. My wife, my oldest son
Liam, and I were driving down Vashti Road around 3:30 p.m. In
front of us was a shiny black hearse and behind us a line of
vehicles as far as you could see. As we looked through the back
glass of that hearse, we saw the small wooden casket with
beautiful flowers resting on top. Within that casket laid one of
the greatest gifts God had ever given to our family. It was our
son Layke. On that Saturday afternoon our journey with Layke
on this earth was coming to an end. That long line of vehicles
which followed behind us included friends and family who had
made the journey alongside Layke and us. However, that journey
was not the ten-mile drive from Calvary Baptist Church where

his funeral was held, but the fourteen-and-a-half-month journey we had been on since the day *Layke Huxton Miller* was born.

To say this journey was an easy one would be a lie. There were times the path was hard and discouraging, but one we do not regret in the least. We traveled it with a child who we know was given to us as a gift. I speak for my wife and myself when I say it was and still is a great honor to be the earthly parents of Layke. When I think of this journey we traveled with Layke, my favorite choir song comes to mind, "Worth Every Mile of the Trip." Truly, being able to travel such a wonderful journey with Layke has been worth it all. There is not one step we regret. If we could go back and do it all over again, we would in a heartbeat. A verse which will be mentioned often in this book is:

> "Every good gift and every perfect gift is from above, and cometh down from the Father of lights."
>
> —James 1:17 KJV

One certainty we have been able to hold to throughout Layke's life and death is that Layke Huxton Miller was a gift from God.

When you look at the gifts God gives, you are looking at an area as broad as the sea. God's gifts come in many different forms and facets. They often come in ways we see, but also come in ways we do not see. God's gifts range from the breath we take, to the money we make. He gives us the gift of physical life and the gift of eternal life. According to Solomon, even our labors are gifts, for he tells us, "to rejoice in his labor; this is the gift of God (Ecclesiastes 5:19, KJV)."

Not only are our labors gifts from God, our rest from our labors is as well, for the Bible tells us that God gave David rest from all his enemies around him (2 Samuel 7:1). To try to name all the gifts God gives is an impossible task. However, the focus of this book is to zero in on one specific gift that God gives, and that is the gift of a child. Throughout the entirety of the Bible God gives children in the form of a gift. Look at Abraham and Sarah, God gave them Isaac as a promised gift to their family. They treated Isaac as a gift from God as well. The very first time we see the word *love* referenced in the Bible is when God recognized Isaac as being the son Abraham: "lovest (Genesis 22:2 KJV)." And when we see barren mothers throughout the Bible God gives them children as *gifts,* as answers to prayers. With mothers like Rachel, or Manoah's wife, or Hannah, we see God gave them each the gift of a child.

Lest we forget, the greatest gift ever given was given in the form of a child, when God sent His only begotten Son to this world in the form of a baby through the virgin womb of Mary.

These children weren't just gifts to their parents, but also gifts to those they would live among. Those barren mothers bore children who would make an impact on the lives of their nations and their generation. Take Rachel, who bore Joseph. He wasn't just a gift to his parents, nor just to his brothers, but Joseph was a gift to all the children of Israel and to all the land of Egypt. Look at Manoah's son Sampson. God used him to deliver the nation of Israel out of the hands of the Philistines. Then look at Samuel as well. He wasn't just a gift to Hannah, but a gift to the entire nation of Israel and he would one day anoint the first two kings who would reign over Israel. Even today children are born as gifts to their families, their churches, their communities, and their countries. So when God gives a gift of a child, he is giving that gift not just to their parents, but to all those around them as well. Candace and I can certainly say that Layke was a gift to us. However, it has been our prayer that his short life would touch many others, and would be considered a gift to all those who came in contact with him.

Layke was a gift to our family and I hope he was a gift to many more as well. God made it clear to us in many ways that Layke truly was a gift given from Him specifically for us. Having that understanding helped us tremendously when we needed it most. I don't think we would have ever grasped hold of that truth if God had not made it evident in many ways, as we will mention a little later. With us knowing Layke was given to us from God, it gave us a pillar to lean on throughout his life. We would lean on it while in the hospital, and we would lean on it when he would fail to thrive in certain areas of life. It would be a stronghold for us when we received discouraging news. When we were standing over his death bed and there was nothing else seemingly to hold on to, we were able to take hold of that and know that God was in the midst of it all.

It also gave us a peace in our hearts. We were able to experience through Layke "the peace of God, which passeth all understanding." Paul goes on to say that it is that peace that "shall keep your hearts and minds through Christ (Philippians 4:7 KJV)." Candace and I can testify that God's peace does pass all our understanding and comprehension. Even in the most painful experiences, knowing the peace of God keeps your heart and your mind. There have been many times where I have wondered how we kept our sanity after seeing the things we did, hearing the things we heard, and having to do the things we did. The only explanation is the peace of God that passes our understanding. It keeps us and secures us when everything else seems to be falling apart.

Having the assurance that Layke was a gift of God also gave us purpose, and let us know Layke had a purpose as well. All children have a purpose, and knowing Layke was given to us from God assured us that there was a purpose in him being our son, and in us being his parents. Paul stated, "For the gifts and calling of God are without repentance (Romans 11:29 KJV)." This simply means that God gives gifts for a reason and he doesn't give them with regret or doubt. He gives gifts *for* a purpose and *on* purpose. There is no gift given from God that is on accident, nor is there any gift given from God that is given to the wrong person. If God gives you a gift, it is because that gift is tailored just for you. When we looked at Layke we knew that God had given him to us *on* purpose and *for* a purpose. Having that assurance that God had a purpose for us and Layke made us strive even more as his parents.

I think about my wife and the countless hours of her doing therapies and staying up late with him so I could go to work. No doubt she did it because she loved him and wanted to, but knowing there was purpose for it all gave us that much more determination to press on. I can't say I did nearly as much as my wife did for Layke. However, I can say that because I knew there was a purpose, it made me stay on my knees in prayer. It made me want to be a better father, and it gave me hope just knowing God had a purpose in giving us Layke. There were times we wondered and still do wonder what God's purpose in giving and taking Layke was and is. One thing we do not doubt is that underneath all we do *not* know, we *do* know there is a purpose and a plan for it all, and that Layke was not given to us in vain.

Knowing Layke was a gift from God gave us a good perspective as well. For there are two perspectives from a human side of things that one can have. Someone can have an *ungrateful* perspective or a *grateful* one. This applies with almost everything in life. Don't get me wrong, it wasn't that we were *thanking* God when we would have to go to the hospital. And most definitely, we were never thanking God for taking our son. However we were able to thank God for giving Layke to us. When we were in the hospital we would thank God for giving him to us as a gift. When we saw his progress and development slow down, sometimes come to a halt or even start regressing, we were still able to thank God for such a precious gift which He had given to us.

The most memorable and difficult moment was when we had to say goodbye, when we thanked God for giving us this amazing gift of Layke. I thought about what Solomon said: "A gift is as a precious stone in the eyes of him that hath it; whithersoever it turneth, it prosereth (Proverbs 17:8 KJV)." That is how we felt about Layke. Wherever we found ourselves with Layke—at home, the hospital, or even standing in the graveyard—we were thankful for him. The only way we were able to have this kind of perspective was to know and understand that Layke was a precious gift to us from God. One thing we all must observe about the gifts of God whatever they may be, is that they are all undeserved. If we earned them or worked for them, then it really wouldn't be a gift. When we looked at our son Layke, we saw a child that we didn't deserve to have in our home. Knowing this made us have a perspective of gratitude and love for him.

Layke was a *peculiar* gift. The word peculiar has two different meanings, either *strange or unusual* or *special or particular*. Layke wasn't strange or unusual in our eyes, but Layke certainly was *special or particular*, and in many different ways. He wasn't the kind of gift someone would ask for on their birthday or Christmas (However, if it were possible we now would ask for Layke at every birthday and Christmas.). Rather, what makes the gifts God gives so *peculiar*—and in my opinion so much better—is that these are often gifts we would never choose for ourselves. I never did pray for God to give our family a child who would have physical difficulties and health complications. I never did pray for God to give our family a child who would only live fourteen and a half months. Those are prayers I never prayed. The prayers I prayed were, "God give us a healthy child." I even prayed and still do pray that God would prosper their lives. However, when we look at what God gave us in Layke we couldn't have asked for a better gift.

Sure, we deeply wish we didn't have to say goodbye and long to hold him and care for him again. But he was a wonderful gift to our home. He brought things to our family we would have never known or experienced. God taught us so much through Layke, which is one reason we have written this book. He was a very peculiar gift. That might not have been the first thought of someone in attendance that sunny Saturday afternoon in November, but it is my prayer that you will see through this book that Layke Huxton Miller was a gift from God above, and from Him alone.

TAYLOR & CANDACE MILLER

Chapter 1:

Before the Gift,
Where James 1:17 Came
Into Our Lives

MANY PEOPLE HAVE what is called a *life verse*. As a Christian others may ask you, "What is your life verse?" When they are asking this they are really wanting to know what your favorite Bible verse is. I remember as a teenager people would ask that question and I would get concerned because at that time I didn't really have a life verse, per se. So I used a verse I had heard other people say was their life verse:

"Trust in the Lord with all thine heart; and lean not unto thine own understanding. In all thy ways acknowledge him, and he shall direct thy paths."

—Proverbs 3:5-6 KJV

This no doubt is a great verse to make your life verse, and is a great verse to base your life around. However, if you were to ask me what my life verse is, I'm not sure I could name one in particular, for there have been many verses that have spoken to me when I needed them in my life. On the other hand, if you were to ask me what our family verse is, I would have no trouble telling you what that verse is. There is one verse that has continually spoken to our lives, even when our family was just in the beginning stages:

"Every good gift and every perfect gift is from above, and cometh down from the Father of lights, with whom is no variableness, neither shadow of turning."

—James 1:17 KJV

On June 21st, 2011 (which was my birthday) I met my wife after a service at the Taylorsville Baptist Camp Meeting. We had messaged back and forth a time or two on Facebook, but had never met in person. She was walking out of the fellowship hall and I was walking in. At that time we spoke for the first time, and she told me she had sang happy birthday to me. That night those who were in the fellowship hall sang happy birthday to the guest preacher that night and to me since he and I share a birthday. Little did I know that was going to lead my wife and me to dating, marriage, kids, and so many wonderful things in this life. Though we met in 2011 we did not marry until 2017. Anyone who knows me, knows that sometimes it takes me longer to get things settled, and at times I can be very indecisive. However, when you are talking about marriage, making a promise to God, and committing the remainder of your life to someone, it is a very serious matter. Whether it takes six weeks, six months, or six years, it is something everyone needs to be sure about and know is the will of God. Although God did not write it in the sky or paint it on a billboard, He did let me know for a fact that Candace Campbell was the one God desired me to share my life with.

As I look back I remember we both prayed for direction concerning our lives and whether or not we were supposed to get married or not. There were struggles at times, and times we wondered what we were supposed to do. Often, I would pray God would give me a wife who would love God more than me, for I knew if she loved the Lord, everything else would fall into place. One evening after church, we went to my Granny's house. Sitting in her driveway, Candace told me she had something she had to share with me. She got in the passenger side of my truck with her Bible in hand. She told me that she had been reading in the book of James and the Lord had spoken to her heart concerning our relationship. At that point I really wasn't sure if I was getting dumped or what was about to happen. But she read James 1:17 to me:

> "Every good gift and every perfect gift is from above, and cometh down from the Father of lights, with whom is no variableness, neither shadow of turning."
>
> —James 1:17 KJV

She told me she knew the "perfect gift" was her salvation, but she said the Lord settled in her heart that the "good gift" was

11

me. It wasn't long after that I knew she was the one for me as well.

It seems very strange to hear myself referred to as a "good gift" from God. I know me—I know all the wrongs, all the flaws, all the bad things about me—and to think that God would reveal to my wife that I was a good gift just doesn't seem right. With that being said, God didn't reveal to me in that moment in time that she was that "good gift" from God for me, but it would soon come.

As stated earlier, I'm sometimes a slow learner and sometimes it takes me much longer to catch on to things, but I can say that God has continually over the four years of our marriage revealed to me that she is a "good gift" from God. I realize that more today than I ever had before. I look at my wife and see how wonderful of a wife and mother she is, and it makes me feel very undeserving. Solomon said,

> "Whoso findeth a wife findeth a good thing, and obtaineth favor of the Lord."
> —Proverbs 18:22 KJV

The word "good" means pleasant, or better. So what Solomon is saying is if God has given you a wife, He has given you something better in life. My life would not be as pleasant and certainly would not be better without my wife by my side. There have been times I have failed to make that recognition, but when I look at some of the places we have had to walk I couldn't imagine walking through them without my wife. Life in itself is hard and presents a lot of challenges and struggles along the way, but doing it alone would be so much harder. God Himself said in the beginning,

"It is not good that the man should be alone."

—Genesis 2:18 KJV

God's remedy for the loneliness of man was a wife. Certainly Candace was a very gracious gift of God to me. If God had not given Candace to me, and me to her, we would have never been able to receive other gifts God had in store for us, especially our two children. Some of the greatest faith-building works God has performed in my life he has through Candace and me as a family. Peter said,

> "Likewise, ye husbands, dwell with them according to knowledge, giving honour unto the wife, as unto the weaker vessel, and as being heirs together of the grace of life."
>
> —1 Peter 3:7 KJV

The word "heirs" speaks of one who obtains something assigned to them. Then the word "grace," speaks of loving kindness and favor. The meaning of all this is that when God pairs a husband and wife, He assigns them for the purpose of showing favor and kindness in their lives.

After we were engaged there were situations concerning where we would live once we got married which God worked out for us. There were also financial situations the Lord provided us for, and so much more. God has done great things for us on the family level, as well as an individual level. This tells me God cares about the family. He cares about the home, and He doesn't just care on a general basis, He cares about your individual family home. It would be very safe to say that family is a "good gift," from God.

In these beginning stages of our family, I see all the ways that God has been faithful to meet our needs and provide for us. It helps me to know He is going to continue to do so in the years to come. Every situation God works out and every prayer God answers are milestones in our lives. They should be as the stones Joshua placed in the Jordan River when they crossed over into Canaan, to remember and lay hold of in future times of trouble. What gets me through hard times is looking back and seeing how God worked and seeing how God prepared us in previous times. I can't remember the man who said it, but a quote that lives true in my heart is,

> "Walking by faith is not walking forward facing forward, but it is walking backward in the forward direction."
>
> —Unknown

When you walk in this manner, you see how God's hand is evident in the path you travel, and you can know that God will be doing the same in the path ahead. God not only works in the present, for the present, but God works in the present, for the preparation of the future as well. There are things God does for us now, to help us down the road. So when God answers a prayer or works a situation out in your life, don't forget it. Let it be a memorial in your heart for what God may be wanting to do later in your life.

Chapter 2:

The Bestowing
of This Gift

"Lo, children are an heritage of the LORD: and
the fruit of the womb is His reward."

—Psalm 127:3

OFTENTIMES UPON HEARING of a mother who is
expecting a child, I think of the verse above. This verse
assures us that the Lord has his hand in the midst of all
that is going on, and He views children as His reward. Along with
this verse there is another verse that comes to mind, and it comes
from the final chapter in the book of Ruth. Ruth and Boaz have
now become married and the Bible says,

"So Boaz took Ruth, and she was his wife: and when he went in unto her, the LORD gave her conception, and she bare a son."

—Ruth 4:13, KJV

The only way conceptions come is if the LORD gives them. This is what makes the birthing of a baby so miraculous. It isn't what we do, but it is the fact that the Lord gives conceptions. What a precious gift God bestows upon us. It amazes me that God would entrust us with gifts he views as "His reward." Children are truly a "good gift, that comes from above."

It wasn't but a few months after we got married and moved into our new home that we found out Candace was pregnant with our first born son, Liam. Liam would be the first everything in our families—first child, first grandchild, and first great grandchild. So needless to say he became a real hit in our family. He has brought and still does bring so much joy to Candace and me. We couldn't even begin to imagine not having him in our home after the passing of our son, Layke. There were many times we were upset thinking about the passing of Layke and Liam would do something that would make us start laughing. Truly, Liam is a gift God has bestowed upon us as well.

While we were enjoying having a family of three, and learning more and more about being parents, Liam's first Christmas was just a couple days away. As a parent, you go above and beyond to make your child's first Christmas special. The ironic thing about that is, a child will never remember their first Christmas. However, it was special for us going and getting gifts for him and hanging a stocking for him, and placing picture ornaments of him on our tree. Candace and I that year made a decision that it would be financially wise for us not to get each other gifts and just focus on getting Liam gifts, and so, that is what we did.

I remember it was three days before Christmas and I was walking through the house with Liam in my arms. I heard Candace call me into the spare bathroom and to my surprise when I walked in she was holding a pregnancy test that had two pink lines.

"I'm pregnant!" she said.

I started walking up and down the hallway carrying Liam singing, "Liam's going to be a brother, Liam's going to be a brother."

This was a total surprise to both of us. I was excited and Candace was saying to herself, "I just had a baby." Of course it is easier for the dad to be excited, we aren't the ones carrying the baby for nine months, and going through labor and delivery.

This was such a surprise to us we couldn't hardly believe it. She had multiple pregnancy tests and began taking them all. Just to make sure those tests weren't shooting off false positives, I decided to take one as well and of course it came back, "not pregnant." Undoubtedly, the Christmas that Candace and I decided to not give gifts to one another, God decided to give us a gift of his own.

We immediately started trying to figure out how we were going to reveal to our families about this new gift we would be receiving. One thing for sure was we wanted it to be as if Liam was the one telling them that he was going to be a big brother. We wanted to do it on Christmas to make it even more special. We looked online for shirts that he could wear and nothing we found would arrive in time, so we decided to get our parents a card and address it from Liam. We wrote the card as if it was Liam telling them. The card read as follows:

" I want to thank you for being such wonderful
grandparents to me. Thank you for all the times
you've made me laugh, took care of me, and most

all, spoiled me to death. I want you to also know this will be the only year that I will be the only grandchild around. YES. I am going to be a big brother! Please make sure this doesn't cause any deductions on my future gifts. I love you, Liam."

We shared it with both of our families. We told my family on Christmas Eve and her family on Christmas Day. It was somewhat funny on Christmas Day, Candace's dad was reading the card aloud from Liam and when he got to the part that revealed Liam was going to be a brother, Liam knocked a cup of coffee off the table onto the floor, breaking the coffee mug and sending glass and coffee everywhere. I guess he wasn't ready to give up all the attention.

After we had announced Candace was expecting, we began planning and trying to get things in order for the arrival of this very unexpected gift that was coming to our home here in a few months. Medical insurance quickly became a priority with the joyous, yet unforeseen news that Candace was expecting. She had recently gone from full-time to part-time hours at work in order to care for Liam, and as a result, would lose access to the medical coverage being offered as a benefit through her employer. Her last day of coverage would be November 30, 2018. We of course quickly began exploring insurance options for Candace. As a result of her having had medical coverage through her employer, continuation coverage (COBRA) was offered, but with her employer no longer contributing to the monthly premiums, COBRA was too costly of an option.

I also checked with my employer, but at the time dependent coverage was not an option. We ended up enrolling her in a limited private policy that went into effect December 1, 2018. We later contacted the carrier only to find that since Candace was expecting prior to the effective date of the policy, maternity coverage would be excluded entirely. We knew then there may be a problem. So we started praying that this conception would be after the 1st of December.

A few weeks later we went to the doctor for her first visit to determine her due date, still praying that it would be after the 1st of December. When the doctor came in, it was actually the very same doctor who delivered Candace as a baby. As we were talking we explained the situation to the doctor and how we were really hoping this date of conception would be after December the 1st. They were not able to determine the due date the way they normally do, which is based on a woman's menstrual cycle. Candace had just had a baby six months earlier and her body wasn't back to normal, so they had to measure the baby to determine the due date via ultrasound. As they measured, the doctor told us November the 8th was the approximate date of conception. This wasn't what we wanted to hear. We knew then we were in a bind, and we were unsure what we needed to do.

After following up with several insurance agents, each confirmed the continuation coverage offered through her employer or a private major medical policy were our only options for her to obtain a plan with maternity coverage. Both were very costly and we didn't want to have to go either of those routes if we didn't have to. We didn't know what we were going to do, but I remember we started praying about the situation and asking God to work it out.

It wasn't but a couple of weeks later Candace's employers came to her and told her that if she would pick up six more hours a week they would consider her full-time and provide her with insurance that would cover the pregnancy. This was a major answer of prayer for Candace and I. Candace had not been at this job long at all, so it wasn't like she had seniority or some kind of pull because she had been there for so long. She was a newbie. It just let us know that when God gives a gift, He works everything out concerning it.

What we came to realize before Layke was even born was that God provides not only the gifts He bestows, but He provides the means to take care and sustain the gifts He gives. There would be many times throughout Layke's life I would look back to God working this out and it would give us encouragement and strength. Seeing God do this for our family helped us realize we could trust God in whatever situation we found ourselves in. Where God gives, He also provides.

Chapter 3:

The Birth of a Gift:
At His Birth

ON WEDNESDAY AUGUST 14th, 2019 I received a call from my wife in the afternoon while at work. She told me she thought she was going into labor and I needed to come on. It was about a twenty-minute drive from work so I was rushing home as fast as I could. When I got there we gathered our things loaded up and headed to the hospital. When we arrived we hurriedly checked in and they took Candace and I back and checked her. She was barely dilated. They decided to give it just a few minutes and they checked again. She was still not really dilated any more. They said she was welcome to walk around and see if anything changed, but most likely this indicated the baby wasn't coming just yet. My wife, being in the medical field and having already had a child, was slightly embarrassed because she didn't want to be one of those mothers who just ran to the hospital every time the baby did something, so she walked around for a while and decided to go back to get checked one more time before we went home. To our surprise, when they checked this time she was dilated more and they decided to admit her that night.

We spent all night in the hospital and I slept in a chair. I wanted to be a good husband who stayed up and was there and attentive but I struggled to stay awake. She woke me up when the anesthesiologist came in to do the epidural, to hold her hand until the doctor was finished. I am pretty sure I dozed off standing there. Morning came and we were still waiting. What was so unique about this was Layke's due date was August 15th and as long as he came before midnight that day he was going to be one of those babies who came on their due date. As the day rolled on, we sat around waiting for Layke to make his entrance into this world. At that time we received one of the greatest gifts we had been given. Candace had felt him kick, hiccup, and roll around within her for months, but at that time we were finally able to see the gift God had given us.

Up until then the only birthing experience I had ever been a part of was when Liam was born. I remember it took about thirty minutes of hard labor, which seemed much longer than that. However when it came time for Layke to be born it was literally a couple minutes and he was here. *This was so easy,* I thought. However, I did not know all that would come to pass. I have always heard of a mother's instinct, but I didn't really believe in it until Layke was born. While everyone was excited and happy he was here, the first words out of Candace's mouth were, "What's wrong?" She immediately knew something wasn't right.

We began looking at Layke along with the doctors and honestly, when I looked at him I felt like something wasn't right either. I mean absolutely no disrespect to my son, but when he was born he didn't look completely healthy. I wasn't sure if it was just because there was swelling around his eyes or whether it was because he was so small. Whatever the reasoning he didn't look like a normal baby and of course, he wasn't. However, when my wife asked what was wrong, the doctor came over and assured her everything was alright. She told her there was nothing that indicated any problems by Layke's physical appearance. So we just thought the concerns we had were false alarms and that as soon as he got over the birthing trauma there would be no concerns. He was born five pounds, two ounces, which we thought was very small, but again the doctors were not concerned. The doctors and nurses did their regular routine, the families came in, and we let people hold him and get their pictures and visit.

As evening approached there began to be small concerns with Layke's health. They kept coming in to get him to check blood sugar, because it continued to drop. It was getting a little worrisome but we knew if something major was going on they would let us know. Eventually, our families went home, and Candace and I were very exhausted.

When Liam was born we decided to let the nurses keep him during the night, we felt that would be the only time our child would have multiple nurses watching him and that would be a great opportunity to get some rest, so we did the very same thing with Layke. We were blessed with an amazing nurse. She treated Candace and me like we were her close friends and treated Layke with such love and care. We felt very comfortable with her watching our child and knew he would be in good hands.

It was about 6:00 a.m. the next morning when the doctor came into the room. She was Liam's pediatrician and now was going to be Layke's as well. I remember her coming in and waking us up. She had a look on her face like she had something she was needing to explain. She began to tell us that Layke's nurse (Lauren) called her in because she was concerned for Layke as he kept spitting up his milk, like he was vomiting. She told us they did some x-rays and there was some concern there was a bowel obstruction, and if this was the case he would be in need of emergency surgery. She told us she had already called Wake Forest Medical Center and they had a transport team already in transit to come get Layke. She also informed us that the surgeons had been consulted as well. She apologized to us that this was going on and that we hadn't had much rest. She assured us they would bring Layke by for us to see him before they took him.

We got up and frantically began to get our things together. We called our families and told them what was going on. I remember being very anxious about seeing Layke and I know Candace was as well, being his mother. When something is wrong with your child you want to be with them and there for them and it was troubling not being able to see him. All the while I was expecting one of the nurses to come carrying him in there, or for them to roll him in on the cart they took him out on. To my shock, they brought him in the incubator in which they transport babies in by ambulance. This incubator looked like a spaceship. It was completely covered in clear glass (or fiberglass) and had wires and tubes running in and out. When I saw that, it felt like my heart sank into my chest. It was as if reality had come and punched me in the stomach. I wasn't expecting that, and I remember I got very scared, because to me that told me how serious things were.

I remember we prayed and asked God to help him and watch over him. As they wheeled Layke out of our room, we began to grab the few remaining items we had in the room, trying our best to hurry. As we were packing, the doctor who delivered Layke just hours prior came into the room. She had consulted with the lab and looked at Candace's placenta and stated that it was the smallest she had ever seen in all her years of delivering. This explained why Layke was so small, he was malnourished due to the small placenta. We asked what this meant and why this happened, and the doctor explained it could mean several things, and of all the possibilities, genetic differences went hand-in-hand with low birth weight. Out of all the reasons she mentioned, that one stood out the most to my wife. The doctor told us if we needed anything to let her know and she left.

When she walked out my mind immediately went back to that night in Carter's baby store when I saw that yellow sticky note that said,

"Every good gift and every perfect gift is from above."

—James 1:17a KJV

I never shared that with my wife. I kept it to myself up until that point and I felt like I needed to share it with her then. Knowing that Layke was a gift from God gave us comfort during that time and let us know God had his hand in the midst of this uncertain situation.

The next time we saw Layke was when we arrived at Brenner Children's Hospital. Fortunately he wasn't in the mobile incubator, he was in a baby bed in the neonatal intensive care unit (NICU). We spent the next week in the hospital. Layke struggled to keep food down for long, but they ruled out any bowel obstruction and felt like he had reflux. This was a relief, and we saw Layke improving some each day, and thankfully, we were able to come home. During this time we saw the importance of family, friends, and a good church. We had people in the waiting rooms every day and night while we were there. This was so encouraging to us, it let us know people cared about us and about Layke. I remember one of Layke's favorite songs came into existence while we were there. Candace's grandmother, Layke's great-grandmother, was holding him and began to sing, "I love little Layke, I do, I do. I love little Layke, I do. I love little Layke,

I do, I do. I love little Layke and Liam too." This would be a song Candace would sing to Layke often throughout his life.

The day finally came when we would be able to bring Layke home. To us it was a sigh of relief. We felt like this had been nothing more than just a bump in the road and God had brought us through it. I remember I was thinking to myself that I would kiss the ground when we got home with Layke. It was hard having our family in three different places every night and I was so excited to be able to have all of us under one roof for the first time. We got everything packed up and started toward home. As we got on 421 North, the entrance ramp looped around and we could see the entire hospital. Candace videoed the hospital and said, "We are finally getting to come home."

Little did we know we would become very acquainted with this place.

Chapter 4:

The Beauty of This Gift

W E ALL KNOW the old saying, "Beauty is in the eyes of the beholder." The truth is, some find beauty in things that others do not. Even though I am careful how I phrase this, there are a lot of things concerning Layke that in the beginning I did not find beauty in. As a matter of fact, there were findings that broke our hearts about Layke, that we now find so much beauty in. I referenced earlier in this book that God gives gifts we would never ask for. Why would I ask God to give us a child with such complications? However, those complications Layke possessed made him all the more beautiful in our eyes.

A week after our son was born, we finally arrived home on a Friday evening to enjoy another precious gift. The following Monday as my wife was preparing to take Layke to his first doctor's appointment, she received a call from a pediatrician at

Brenner Children's Hospital. While we were in the NICU the previous week my wife requested genetic testing of Layke due to the complications that had arisen so quickly in Layke's short life. In addition to those obstacles he had already faced, my wife was concerned shortly after his birth when she was informed the placenta was abnormally small. The doctor who delivered Layke stated there could be many reasons for that, including genetic disorders.

During Layke's hospital stay, we received the results back for one of the genetic tests called a *karyotype*[1]. This particular test checked to make sure Layke had all the proper amount of chromosomes within his DNA. The doctor told us generally if this test comes back normal, then most likely the next one will as well. At that point we were not super concerned about his genetics after receiving this encouraging news.

The Monday after arriving home my wife received the results of the second genetic test, called a *microarray analysis*[2]. I can still hear the fear and anxiety in Candace's voice, as she proceeded to tell me there were abnormalities present in this test. The doctor was unable to give us a detailed explanation of what these findings really meant because she was not the genetic specialist relaying the results. (If you can only imagine this fearful news, compounded by the unknown of what it all meant.) She stated we would need to see our pediatrician, and they would refer us

---

[1] A karyotype is a preparation of the complete set of metaphase chromosomes in the cells of a species or in an individual organism, sorted by length, centromere location and other features. and for a test that detects this complement or counts the number of chromosomes. —Wikipedia

[2] A microarray analysis compares a person's DNA to "control DNA". The control DNA comes from a person that doesn't have a chromosome abnormality. A chromosome change is identified when there are differences between a person's DNA and the control DNA. — https://www.chromosome18.org

to the geneticist at Brenner Children's Hospital where we could discuss the matter further.

As my wife hurriedly prepared to take our son to his appointment, all she could think was, *What does this mean for our son and his future?*

I met Candace and Layke at the pediatrician's office, hoping we would receive a better explanation of these abnormal findings. Layke's pediatrician confessed she wasn't as familiar with this particular genetic disorder, and her information was limited. What we did know was that Layke had a difference in DNA called *Xq28 duplication syndrome*[3]. This is a genetic duplication involving the X chromosome of the q28 region. This sounded like Greek to my wife and me, and we were told this syndrome came with many disabilities for our son, including chronic infections. We set up our consultation with the geneticist at Brenner Children's Hospital and were scheduled to go that following Friday.

The time that passed until we met with the geneticist were stressful and worrisome hours. All this uncertainty had been dropped upon us and we were left feeling helpless. My wife and I began looking online to try and understand this condition, and quite frankly it was very scary. Life expectancy was as short as twenty-five years old. There were physical signs Layke was already presenting. The internet predicted seizures would be frequent in his life. But the most alarming thing was that a child would often fail to thrive and would struggle keeping food down. This was the very reason he was sent to Brenner Children's NICU in the first place. Uncertainty and fear took hold of us, the fear gripping our hearts, scared of what the consultation with the genetic doctor would reveal.

---

[3] Xq28 duplication syndrome is an X-linked intellectual disability syndrome characterized by variable degrees of cognitive impairment (typically more severe in males), a wide spectrum of neurobehavioral abnormalities, and variable facial dysmorphic features. —https://www.ncbi.nlm.nih.gov

Our appointment was soon approaching that Friday. I attended our weekly prayer meeting that Tuesday night prior. Our pastor was away preaching a revival and I had to moderate the service that night while another young preacher preached. During the service all I could think about was all that was going on in our family. There were only a handful of people who knew of our situation. However, there was one lady in our church who had no idea what we were dealing with at the time. She stood up in the middle of the service as a group was singing and came up to the pew I was sitting on. She handed me a badge that said, "God's Got This." She told me she wanted to bring it to the hospital while Layke was in the NICU, but failed to do so. She said she wasn't even going to give it to me now, because she thought everything was better with Layke, but the Lord kept dealing with her heart about gifting us the pin, so she did.

God knew exactly when I needed that and assured me He knew where my family was and knew what we were facing. To this day, I think about that small act of kindness, and it touches me to know that the Lord knows when we need assurance.

The following Friday came and we journeyed to Brenner Children's Hospital for our consultation. Candace, her mother, Layke, and I attended. Our appointment was the last of the day so we could have extended time if needed. We had previously heard about the genetic doctor we would soon meet as many had spoken highly of her. When we met her, we immediately recognized that she had a wonderful personality and an overwhelming love for children with special needs. We introduced ourselves and began talking about Layke. We received a crash course on genetics and then went over Layke's DNA and what was unique about his situation.

Candace and I had never experienced anything of this nature before. I looked out the window of the room and noticed how bright the sun was shining. Inside our hearts was a dark cloud as we began to hear some of the many struggles that Layke could possibly face in life. The doctor informed us Layke's condition was a very rare disorder and there had only been two hundred recorded cases in the world. If you do the math, the odds of a child being born with Xq28 duplication syndrome are very close to impossible, even across the world's population. We heard things that day such as he may never walk or talk in this life, or he may start walking at some point and then get to where he is unable. We heard his muscle strength would go from very loose and low muscle tone to severely tight and spastic, impairing his mobility. Other complications included a compromised immune system, frequent respiratory infections, and severe mental disability. This was a very hard pill to swallow.

I remember sitting there and it was all I could do to keep from breaking down in tears in that room. I looked over at my son and my heart broke because I didn't know what life would look like for him. These are the last words you want to hear concerning your child. My lip quivered and my eyes filled with tears. I couldn't say a word, because I knew the moment I tried to speak it would all pour out.

It amazed me how well my wife kept things together during that appointment. She maintained a clear mind and asked difficult questions (and she continued to advocate for Layke in the same manner throughout his entire life). She wanted to know the clinical picture of who Layke was and what he would be. We left that day with a lot of answers, but there was a lot left unanswered in our hearts and minds. As we walked out of the hospital that day the thought came to me once again,

> "Every good gift and every perfect is from above."
>
> —James 1:17a KJV

I knew as impossible as the odds seemed, with only two hundred recorded cases, Layke was no accident. It was not by coincidence this child had been given to us, but he was part of God's divine plan.

Upon returning home that evening, we informed our families of the discouraging doctor's appointment that revealed the prognosis we were given for Layke. I called a close pastor friend of mine and told him all that we had heard. He made a statement to me that day that changed my whole perspective about Layke. He told me, "Layke would be Layke. He will be exactly like he is supposed to be."

For the previous few days all I could think about was that Layke would be hindered by these challenges. I thought behind those problems was a normal, healthy child who couldn't be himself. However, after that conversation, I knew that wasn't the case. David said,

"I will praise thee; for I am fearfully and wonderfully made."
—Psalms 139:14a KJV

He went on to say a few verses later,

"How precious also are thy thoughts unto me, O God! How great is the sum of them."
—Psalms 139:17 KJV

Layke was formed and made by God Almighty, the exact way he was made to be. However, it wasn't just Layke formed in this fashion, but you and I are as well, along with any child conceived. I was afraid I may never know who my son really was or supposed to be until these words spoke to my heart, letting me know Layke was made perfect according to God's plan for who he was supposed to be.

Soon we would take Layke to church for the first time. We were nervous, it seemed like life had been shaken up for us the past several weeks. We feared taking him out for the risk that he might get sick or catch something because of his immune disorder. However, we believed and still do today that it is important to take your children and your family to the House of God. So by faith, we took him for the first time and I will never forget what our pastor preached that Sunday. The title of his message was "In the Lord Put I my Trust." His message came from Psalms chapter 11. Though I cannot remember everything he said in that message, I do remember him expounding upon a phrase found in verse 4, where David says,

> "his eyes behold, his eyelids try, the children of men."
>
> —KJV

He illustrated that phrase as one reading the fine print and having to pull the book or page up close to focus on it. The Lord spoke to my heart as my family of four sat on the pew that day. The Lord assured me He was focusing on what we were going through and he had His hand on Layke.

As a parent, you want what is best for your children. Though we knew God gave him to us with a purpose, we also knew he was fearfully and wonderfully made by God. We still prayed for God to touch Layke and heal his body. However, you may wonder why the title of this chapter is "The Beauty of this Gift." All these difficulties Layke possessed made him beautiful. I sit here today and will admit I don't regret praying those prayers for God to touch and heal my son. However, I do wish I would have taken more time thanking God for this beautiful gift, rather than continuously asking God to change this gift. For now as we look back, it was those struggles that made Layke all the more beautiful in our eyes. The Bible teaches us that our days are numbered. When Layke was born on August the 15th, 2019, God had already set a date on November 4th, 2020 that he would take him home. All these things that appeared to be as struggles in one sense, now appear as blessings in disguise.

Layke's struggles demanded we as parents spend even more time with him. The fact that he couldn't walk, crawl, feed himself, or really sit up independently meant he needed one of us to be there nearly all the time. If Layke went from one room to the next it was because we had carried him there. These struggles forced us to hold him more than a normal child. In the last months he was alive, one of the most beautiful sights was watching Layke get excited. I could make my hand into a claw and slowly bring it down to him and he would anticipate it coming and start kicking and flailing his arms because of his excitement. Also, Layke enjoyed when we laid him down and threw a blanket over him, then quickly yanked it away. He would let out the sweetest squeal and cackle. It was so beautiful watching him. His mind was very delayed, so we don't know how much he really comprehended, but even that aspect made him beautiful.

Anything Layke learned to recognize was astounding to us whereas if a normal, healthy child would do this we would likely just expect and overlook it. That was not the case with Layke.

One thing he paid close attention to was his food. When Candace or I would make a bottle in the kitchen we often would tilt the reclining chair back and sit Layke in it until the bottle was ready. As we walked into the kitchen, we would see his little head, with messed up hair slowly begin to turn and look our way to watch us. He knew we were making his food and he would sit in anticipation waiting for it. Also, in those last months Layke started to learn his name, and we could be in the same room and start calling, "Layke," or I would say, "Laykeums," and that head would slowly turn in the direction we were calling from. These little delays that seem so small and insignificant, many may over look, but we were able to see great beauty in them.

If you have kids, you know they tend to have their favorite people. They go through phases of who they favor. I would have to say that Layke's favorite person was his Mama. However, other than his Mama, Layke didn't have favorites. If you wanted to hold Layke, he would love for you to. I've never seen a more content child than him. You could hold and kiss him as long as you wanted. The times he cried was when he was hungry or if his stomach was hurting. During those times he could throw a fit with the best of them.

One of the first traits that stood out to us about Layke was his grip. Even days after he was born we noticed he had a strong grip for such a small child. He would grip your finger and squeeze. Then as life went on we found out he would grip anything he could get a hold of, whether it was your hand, your hair, or your ear. He even went to the point he would grab ahold of our dog, Dolly's hair. He had a very strong grip. While that was the first thing we noticed about Layke, it also was the last thing we noticed as well, especially during those fleeting final moments of his life. We held him in our arms as they were taking him off life support. As they began to cut those machines off, Candace was holding his hand. The last thing we noticed was that grip as he gripped her hand for the final time. Oh what we would give to feel that grip one more time.

Layke was a beautiful gift that was given to us, and what is so amazing is the next time we see him, he will be more beautiful than before. We long to see our beautiful gift again.

Chapter 5:

The Burden of This Gift

A S YOU LOOK at the title of this chapter, don't get the wrong impression when I use the term, "burden." There are burdens in life we despise and wish we could do without, such as taxes, bills, and other things of that degree. However, in life and especially in the Christian journey there are burdens we gladly carry. Layke most certainly was one of those burdens we were glad to carry. It was an honor to do what we were able to do for him in his short lifetime.

One may ask, "Was the burden heavy at times?"

We would have to answer, "Yes." There were many times it wasn't easy, but there never came a time we didn't want to carry it. Truly, the burden we have carried without Layke has been much heavier and harder than the burden we carried with him. Whatever this amazing gift brought to us, we were willing to carry it, not only because it was our duty and responsibility as parents, but because we loved the gift God had graciously blessed us with.

Any time God gives a gift, it comes with burdens. There are many people God has gifted in many ways, but along with that gift comes burdens of responsibility and accountability. You see, when God gives a gift, we must give account for how we handled it. I think of those God has given the talents to sing or play instruments. With those gifts come hours of practice and preparation. I myself have been given the call to preach, and with that calling comes burdens. Even our greatest gift in this life— our salvation—comes with burdens. To be honest, if it is a true gift from God it will come with a burden. Every honest parent must step back and admit that if God has given them the gift of a child, He also has given them a burden to go along with the child.

Burdens Bring Pain

When you look at the burdens that come along with the gifts God gives, they are also accompanied by pain and heartache. I have found that no one has a more direct avenue to your heart than your family, especially your children. This was no exception with Layke. From the time my wife and I found out we were expecting, Layke had our hearts and still does today. It saddened us as his parents to watch him struggle to carry out simple tasks, such as holding a toy and bringing it to his mouth, sitting up, swallowing correctly, and learning to speak. As a parent you want to see your children thrive and succeed in everything they do. It was difficult watching him strive to overcome these struggles, but many times fail.

Regardless of the difficulty that came with these simple tasks, Layke continued to put his best effort in trying to succeed. He was a fighter and very determined, despite all the setbacks that came his way. My heart ached for Layke while he was in the hospital and required oxygen, nasogastric tubes, and many other assistive medical devices. Many times I thought of my children's futures and ached to imagine Layke watching his older brother Liam and other children succeeding at activities he physically couldn't do. My mind would skip forward in life to a future ballgame that our family would attend, supporting Liam as he played and Layke having to watch. Those thoughts brought tears to my eyes, just thinking of them and knowing this may never be possible for Layke.

We always made Layke a part of everything we did even though many times it was brought to our attention that Layke may never have the opportunity to participate in the activities others around us enjoyed. These burdens were made real in our lives because one of life's greatest joys is seeing your children succeed.

Burdens Bring Pleasure

I can't speak for anyone else, but there is a sense of fulfillment when carrying a burden. One of the most beautiful things you will ever see is someone carrying a burden they are glad to carry. I still look back on pictures and videos of my wife doing therapies with Layke. I did them with him at times, but for the most part she took this burden on. She would do them every day, sometimes twice per day. This would be very time consuming and require her focus. It wasn't something she could do while multitasking. Due to Layke's weakness and physical dependence on others, this would demand her undivided attention. However, when I look at those pictures and videos of her doing those therapies, there was always a smile on her face. She loved working with him and watching him progress, while faithfully cheering him on.

There were many times he would regress or his progress would come to a halt, but she continued to push him toward success. This was a burden that brought pleasure to my wife. Still to this day, she wishes she could get down on the floor with him and let him prop sit, or put his braces on his chunky little feet, and let him bear weight. This was a burden she gladly carried for Layke. There is no greater fulfilment in life than carrying a burden in the will of God, and seeing it pay off. One thing my wife loved was sharing the victories Layke had and watching him slowly, but surely make progress.

Burdens Bring You Many Places

The burdens that accompany the gifts of God will oftentimes lead you to places you would've never been, if not for the providence of God. I began to reflect on the various places Layke's life led my wife and me. We would not have become acquainted with places such as Brenner Children's Hospital or the Ronald McDonald House. Were these places we desired to go for pleasure? Absolutely not, but we were guided to these places on a mission to seek help and answers for our precious son. In all reality, these places were blessings in disguise where medical professionals would tenderly care for our sick son, and places where we could find physical rest away from the hospital. Notice, we were not led to these places just in passing. However, the Lord had Layke in these places to make an impact on certain individuals for a purpose. We failed at times to be the witness we should have been, but the Lord opened many doors for us to testify of God's goodness and His faithfulness. Every place the Lord took Layke, it was our privilege to be at his side each step of the way. Better yet, it thrills my soul that one day we are going to be able to go to another place where our son is waiting. This is only made possible because of the gift of eternal life, not through my son Layke, but through God's Son, Jesus Christ.

Burdens Bring Many People

The Bible says,

> "Bear ye one another's burdens, and so fulfill the
> law of Christ."
>
> —Galatians 6:2 KJV

It was amazing to us how many people drew near to our
family during the course of Layke's life. For us to say we did
everything on our own would be a lie. God placed people in our
lives to help us, and more importantly to be there for Layke.

Very early on in Layke's life he began receiving various types
of therapy, from physical therapy to occupational therapy. Every
week we would have one, two, and sometimes three therapists in
our home working with Layke. These ladies were absolutely
tremendous at what they did, not just in the therapy they
provided, but also in the care and support they showed Layke.
They were so encouraging and optimistic with Layke. At each
session I had the privilege to be a part of, my spirits were lifted
to witness this. They pushed him, cheered for him, and rejoiced
with him every time he would reach a milestone. As a parent, it
was very rewarding to have people such as this in my child's life.

Not only did Layke have a good therapist, but he had good
friends as well. In burdensome times you recognize the
importance of good friends. The Lord placed special people in
our lives to help Layke and us. There were so many that prayed
for him and wanted to be a part of his life because of the special
person he was.

I firmly believe God puts people in specific churches for a
reason. Layke was placed in Calvary Baptist Church with a
purpose and a plan. This church helped my family throughout

Layke's life, as well as his death. In my personal opinion, he could not have been placed in a better church. The people of Calvary Baptist Church loved and cared for Layke throughout the entirety of his life. Each time we were in the hospital my wife and I would receive an innumerable amount of texts and calls from the people of our church. They would call or text to simply remind us they were there for us and were holding our family up in prayer.

Many times, Layke's hospital admissions led to me missing work throughout the week. As a father and primary provider for my family, this placed a heavy weight on my shoulders because of the financial strain it caused. But I say that to say this: Every time Layke was admitted into the hospital we ended up having more money given to us than if I was working my normal full-time schedule. The majority of the time, it was the people of our church who made this possible. We are forever grateful for this blessing. Only my God can make miracles such as this come to pass. Not only our own church, but other churches bound together and prayed for our son, as well as helped us during difficult times. Layke was loved by the people of God, and truly the church helped carry his burdens.

Layke was not only given a good church, but he was given a great pastor as well. He was there when Layke was taken to the neonatal intensive care unit (NICU) at Brenner Children's Hospital the day after he was born, and he was there in the pediatric intensive care unit (PICU) when he took his last breath on this side. He was also present at each admission between his first and last hospital stay. Sometimes it is just one's presence that offers the most comfort.

Our pastor went above and beyond to be there for Layke, as well as our family. Not only was he there for Layke, but he prayed for him on a daily basis. For most people, the only way you may know they are praying for you is if they tell you. However, he didn't have to tell me. I had the privilege of hearing him pray for my son. My pastor and I met nearly every morning throughout the week and prayed together for several years. There were mornings when I was discouraged about the circumstances my family and I were dealing with, whether they concerned setbacks Layke was facing or simply what his future may hold. However, as we met to pray, I could hear him across the room crying out Layke's name in prayer. What an encouragement and comfort to know someone was praying for my son.

There will be times in life when we need help with the burdens we carry. Thank the Lord for a pastor who was faithful to help carry Layke's burden. Needless to say, Layke was blessed with a wonderful pastor.

Layke had a wonderful family surrounding him, but also to help carry his burdens. To mention them all would be impossible. From grandparents, aunts, uncles, great-grandparents, and cousins, they all cared for Layke. They helped in many different ways by offering their services to be a blessing. For example, when Layke was born he was unexpectedly small and needed preemie clothes instead of newborn sizes. My wife and I did not prepare for such a small child, being he was born on the due date we were given and no doctor had predicted for him to be a smaller birth weight. However, in this situation, our family gladly went out and bought Layke many clothes to wear in the size he needed. This is a small act of kindness, but it meant a lot to my wife and me because we had many other worries concerning his health soon after he was born.

There were also times while in the hospital we would be out of work. Once again our family stepped in and paid for some of our bills, fed our dog, mowed our lawn, and took care of our oldest son Liam. In various ways they bore the load and did anything needed for us. Each week Candace's mother was there and helped with Layke's therapies, or the therapist came to her house if we were working. There was always someone there in our family to pick up the load when we couldn't do it all.

43

Our pastor made a statement at Layke's funeral I feel was very true. He stated, "When one got tired, there was another in line waiting to hold him."

I also stated at Layke's funeral, "Anytime Layke was admitted to the hospital, you could guarantee there was a waiting room full of family that loved him. Many times with visitor restrictions they wouldn't all get to see him. However, they were there to show their love and support no matter what. Layke had many family members cheering him on. In fact, the waiting room was always full. I'm sure the hospital was glad to see Layke recover just so that the entourage of people in his family wouldn't be filling the waiting rooms up."

That 4th of July we returned from vacation and Layke started getting sick. He seemed very congested, lethargic, and had a decrease in appetite. So that night around 9:00 p.m. we took him to the emergency room at Brenner Children's Hospital. We were in the ER until probably 2:00 a.m. that next morning. After working him up, they diagnosed him with pneumonia and dehydration, and wrote him a prescription for an antibiotic to take while at home. While we were in the ER I sent my grandmother a text message asking her to pray for Layke, and that we were at the hospital. Little did my grandmother know, we had been sent home by the time she saw the message the very next morning. She drove an hour to the hospital to be there for Layke, and realized only later he had been discharged around 2:00 a.m. that morning. I woke up the next day to several texts and missed calls from my grandmother.

This is just one instance of how Layke's family carried his burdens. At the drop of a hat if Layke needed anything, there would be a line of people there to help us. To try to pen everything Layke's family did would be virtually impossible because the list would be too long. However, what made it clear Layke had a wonderful family was watching them as we said goodbye to this gift. Our family was devastated. It was very visible, the hurt in our family's heart, when Layke passed. Everyone missed helping bear Layke's burdens. Like Candace and me, our family would do anything to help carry them again. To say the least, Candace and I could have never made it through carrying these burdens by ourselves, and we are grateful God put a wonderful family to stand by us.

One of Layke's biggest encouragers was his brother Liam. Liam would always call Layke "Brudder," and he still does today. Liam and Layke were fifteen months apart, so very close in age. Throughout Layke's life, it was a blessing to watch Liam be there and want to help carry his brother's burdens. There were so many times Liam would just out of the blue embrace Layke and give him a big hug and kiss on the head, while telling him he loved him. Whenever Layke would excel in his therapies or perform an exercise, often Liam would say, "Way to go Brudder."

Layke had an *exersaucer*, much like a stationary walker where Layke's feet would touch the floor to bear his very light weight. Surrounding him there were toys Layke could play with using his hands. We would place him in this if we had to get ready or if there was something in the house we had to take care of. If Liam was being mischievous or starting to get into things he shouldn't, we would tell him we needed him to go check on "Brudder," and with excitement he would take off toward the living room to go see what Layke was doing. Once he checked on him, he would run back to us and say, "He's playing with toys." He enjoyed playing with and helping Layke in any way he could.

The most significant thing Liam would do for Layke was pray for him. There were many times Layke had a hard time progressing in his therapies and it seemed as if things were getting worse. It was very discouraging as a parent. During those times we would ask Liam if he could go pray for his brother. Most of the time he would take off over to our brick fireplace, get down on his knees and say, "God is great, God is good, help Brudder, amen." Immediately after praying he would get up and turn around and ask, "Is he better?" He believed that immediately after one prays, things change. I hope he never loses that belief, that God answers prayer, and prayer does change things. For there were many times we saw God answer the prayers of a little child praying for his brother.

When I think of Liam helping carry Layke's burdens, my mind always goes back to the Saturday before Layke was born. We were on the floor of my study, reading the Bible to Liam. Weeks prior we had started reading the book of Proverbs, and our goal was to finish it before Layke was born. That day we came to chapter 17, and as we were reading we read across this verse:

"A friend loveth at all times, and a brother is born for adversity."

—Proverbs 17:17 KJV

When we read that verse, the Lord touched my heart, and I vividly remember reading it again. In my mind I thought the Lord was telling us that Layke was going to be there for Liam's adversity, but soon after Layke's arrival, we realized life was going to present a lot of struggles for Layke. It was made clear to me that God showed us that verse because Liam would be present through Layke's adversity. Even for such a young child, Liam truly helped bear the burdens Layke had.

Burdens Bring You to Prayer

As I look back, one result in carrying this burden with Layke, is that it brought us to prayer. I don't think we would have ever prayed as fervently as we did if it wasn't for carrying this burden. As I mentioned earlier in the book, we would try to read a chapter or two out of the Bible each night, and then we would gather around our brick fireplace and pray. I remember one night we were sitting on the couch. We had just finished reading and we were all sleepy and ready for bed. I told Candace we would just pray there on the couch. Liam perked up and said, "No, we pray over there," and pointed to the fireplace. So we got up and went and prayed over the brick fireplace as we always had.

On a serious note, we didn't know what Layke's future would look like, nor did we know what life would bring his way. One thing we didn't want was for us to look back and say we failed to pray for our children, especially for Layke. It may be selfish of us but most of our prayers did center around Layke. The more I look back, I don't feel bad at all about that, because he was given to us by God, and the burden that came along with Layke drove us to our knees many times. One prayer we prayed for him daily was that God would give him legs that would walk, a tongue that could talk, and a mind that could think clearly. I really felt like the Lord would answer that prayer at some time or another in Layke's life. God did answer that prayer even though it wasn't the way we had envisioned it. I thought there would come a day when we would see him take his first step and we would hear him say his first word. Those thoughts excited me.

On November 4th, 2020 around 2:30 p.m. that afternoon, Layke took his first step and spoke his first words. However, his first steps were not taken on the dust of this sin-cursed world, but they were taken on streets of purest gold. Although he never spoke a word in the stammering tongue of this life, on that day he spoke with another tongue, whether he joined in with singing, shouting, or saying "Alleluia," with the multitude that John saw in Revelation chapter 19. I'm not sure what he did, all I know is that he had a tongue that loosed to praise the Lord.

We always wondered what he really knew and understood in this life. Even though we can never be sure what he knew then, he knows much more now in Heaven than we would ever be able to know in a thousand years of this life. The burden of prayer was a burden that was gladly carried with this gift.

Burdens Bring Provisions

The gifts God gives do come with burdens, but those burdens don't come without provisions. God provided for our family during Layke's life in many different ways, but two ways in particular always come to my mind. As stated, there was a financial burden that came along with this gift. With Candace working only once a week, it left me to be the sole provider for our family. There were times we just simply couldn't afford to go places or buy things. Anyone who has a child knows the two biggest and continual expenses with a baby are diapers and food. We rarely had to buy either for Layke. I think of my grandmother, who almost every time she came to our house brought a big box of diapers and wipes with her. That was one way how God provided for us with the burdens that came along with Layke.

Another way God provided was with the formula that Layke was required to drink. When we discovered Layke had a milk allergy, he was only a couple of months old. This required him to consume a special kind of formula. The formula was exactly what he needed, however it was double the cost of ordinary baby formula. Across the entire fourteen months we only bought one can of this specialty formula out of our own pockets. There was a lady whose daughter was friends with Candace and her sister. She reached out to my wife right when we needed it most, and offered to provide this formula through the company she worked for. There were times we walked out on our porch and there sat a box of formula that would last Layke a couple of weeks, and there were other times we would get a text message saying she sat some formula out on her porch for us to pick up on our way home. Every time I found a box of formula on our porch, my mind always ran to the Brook Cherith[4], where God fed Elijah. Every morning and every evening God sent provisions for him (1 Kings 17).

There is no telling how much money we did not have to spend, solely due to these two acts of kindness shown to us. There may be burdens with your gift, but there are always provisions that come with those burdens.

God's gifts come with burdens, but along with those burdens, God gives us what we need to help bear those burdens. As stated at the beginning of this chapter the burdens of this gift were gladly borne, not just by us but by many others as well. We sincerely miss carrying these burdens.

---

[4] Cherith A small brook flowing into the Jordan, to which Elijah once withdrew, and where ravens brought him supplies of bread and flesh, 1 Kings 17:3-5. Robinson suggests that it may be the present Wady Kelt, which drains the hills west of Jericho, and flows near that town on its way to the Jordan. This brook is dry in summer. —https://biblehub.com

Chapter 6:

The Bliss of This Gift

I REALIZE THERE has been a lot of discussion within this book concerning the burdens that come along with the gifts God gives His children. I would not dare say that these gifts only accompany burdens. For that is not all that follows a gift. Also, I have discussed how the gifts God gives are not always the gifts we would ask for or desire. However, the gifts God gives, oftentimes are very blissful. In so many ways, I have witnessed the blessing and bliss outweigh the burdens, by far. God gives us gifts for our enjoyment and our pleasure in this life. My wife and our family experienced this firsthand when the Lord gave us Layke. Layke being exactly who he was, made him a very enjoyable gift to our home. Looking back on it now there were some things about Layke that made him more enjoyable *with* all the struggles he had. In this chapter I want to look at those blissful attributes of Layke.

His Contentment

Layke was a very content baby. As mentioned previously, the only times he really got upset was if he was hurting or hungry. You never had to worry about Layke throwing a fit due to the lack of attention he was getting. He would be just as content with a toy or without a toy. He was content whether you were playing with him or you weren't. This attribute made Layke all the more enjoyable. The fact that he was content, just made one want to hold and hug him more.

Likewise, because he didn't demand as much attention as your typical child to be happy, it drove one to want to give him attention even more. I always loved to watch Layke sleep. He would lay there on his side and snooze away with his little arms and hands curled under his chin. He always slept with his eyes halfway open for some reason. However, most kids when they wake up from a night's sleep or a nap normally demand attention, and do so by crying once they wake. Our oldest son Liam, when he wakes up and someone isn't in there, often starts hollering, "Daddy, Mommy, come here." When Layke woke up, he normally lied there silently and looked around so sweetly.

His Chair

Our home is full of blissful memories of Layke. There are certain places Layke would be most times in our home. Sometimes he would be in the floor under his jungle gym, while other times he would be in his exersaucer or highchair. However, there is one particular place that always reminds us of Layke, and it is still there today. We have a recliner in our living room a man bought for us when we moved into our new home. That was considered my chair when we first received it. (It seems as though every man has their own personal chair.) Although the chair was originally mine, over time it became Layke's chair. We could recline that chair slightly and Layke would fit in it just perfectly. There was no risk of him falling out or rolling out. He would sink back into the back of that chair and sit there. In that chair he would watch whatever was on TV, which was mostly YouTube videos Liam liked, or gospel music videos.

Oftentimes when we would fix him a bottle he would wait patiently in that chair while we were making it. He had the perfect view into the kitchen. I can still see that shining face turning toward the kitchen with his big blue eyes fixed on whoever was making his bottle of milk. It would always thrill my wife and me, seeing him comprehend something like that.

That chair was a place where Layke was held and rocked to sleep many nights. It was a chair where Layke was tickled, and many sweet cackles rang from his voice. Many books were read to our son in that chair, and many songs were sung to him. However, now when we look at that very chair our minds wander to all those blissful memories that surround it. To this day, we still refer to that chair as Layke's chair.

His Cuddles

My wife and I both agree that Layke was one of the best cuddlers. When I held Layke, I always put his face close to mine. I kissed his head and loved feeling his hair on my face. When he was content he laid in your arms and cuddled with you as long as you desired. Layke never got his mind on anything else or took his attention elsewhere.

There were many times I watched my wife cuddle with Layke as well, and I could see how much she loved doing this. She would place Layke's face right against hers, rub his golden blonde hair, and kiss his forehead. Many times he would gently take one hand and slowly raise it to place it on your cheek. He would then proceed to rub your face with his chunky little hand and lock eyes with you so innocently. My wife would smile back at him each time. His gentle spirit and loving personality made him easy to cuddle with, and make precious memories such as these.

His Correction

One of the hardest roles, I have realized, in parenting is correcting your child when it is needed. Surprisingly, Layke was a child we never had to call down, correct, or discipline in any way. My wife was doing a questionnaire for a program Layke was involved in. The case manager was asking questions to gain a better understanding of our son's development. She wanted to know how Layke responded to being told "no." Candace responded, "I can't answer that because I have truly never had to tell him no." Layke was as innocent as he could be. He was a child we never had to correct in any way, and a gift that was so unique and special.

His Countenance

As I look back on memories we have and all the pictures taken of Layke, there is something that stands out to me above everything else. Layke's facial expressions were another attribute that set him apart. If you look at a picture of him smiling, he had a soft, sweet smile that would melt your heart. His smile had the ability to light up a room. It was so captivating. When Layke smiled we always stopped what we were doing and focused on that. When Layke was a newborn, my wife would worry many times because it took him so long before we ever witnessed his smile. She would cry at times wondering if he would ever be able to, due to his genetic difference. As a parent, you desire to see that expression come across your child's face, because all you want for their life is happiness and success. We had watched him struggle in many different aspects with his health, but when he finally smiled our world stopped. His smile is something we miss dearly and often reminisce on these precious moments.

His Cackles

It wasn't just his smile that warmed our hearts, but we loved to watch his face as he got excited. If we found something that made him excited, we did it over and over again just to hear his laugh. Candace had a way of tickling him and he would just laugh and cackle. I always loved giving him the claw. I would start way up high and slowly bring it to him to tickle him. As my hand approached him, he would get so excited and try to block my hand and his face would just make the most excited expression. It was something I did over and over again, because I loved the thrill it gave him. There were also times he would be lying down and we would take a blanket and throw it over him and then jerk it up. As the blanket lifted from his face, he would let out a high-pitched squeal or laugh.

These are precious memories to us. The reason they are so fond to our hearts is because we knew that there were a lot of days that were tough for him, days he didn't smile and didn't laugh, because of struggles he faced. One joy we have in all of this, is knowing he is in a place where there is no crying, where there is no pain or suffering. I'm completely convinced that in the presence of our Lord, there is a sweet smile on our child's face. We long to see that sweet smile again.

With Layke, we were able to experience such joy and happiness, although a lot of his life was full of heartache, sickness, pain, and difficulty. The bliss we experienced with Layke was even more special to us because those struggles made us enjoy the smiles and laughs so much more. It caused us to cherish those joyful moments and sketch them in our minds. Those times of happiness we experienced with Layke far outweighed the hard times. I can truly say that all the struggles that came along with Layke's life were worth it, just to have experienced the bliss and happiness we did while he was ours for a short while.

Chapter 7:

The Brevity of This Gift

"Whereas ye know not what shall be on the morrow. For what is your life? It is even a vapor that appeareth for a little time, and vanisheth away."

—James 4:14 KJV

ONE CERTAINTY THAT we all know, but never seem to get a hold of, is that tomorrow is not promised, and all we really have is today. This became a challenging reality for us with Layke when he took his last breath on Earth. I'm grateful for the gifts of God that are eternal, gifts like our salvation in Christ, and our home in Heaven that has been saved for us. However, there are many gifts God gives that are not eternal. Gifts that are only afforded to us for a short while. There are many people who get up every day with an arsenal full of God's gifts. We have been given life, health, and strength. God has given us jobs to provide for our families and the ability to do those jobs. God has given family and friends we love and who love us. The list can go on and on of all that God has graciously given. Sadly, many of us fail to take full advantage of them, much less thank God for them. We must come to the realization that in a moment, all of these blessings can be taken from us.

I can't help but think of Job. One day Job got up and had his family, his wealth, his health, and much more. However before the day ended Job had none of these (Job 1-2). All had been taken from him.

My wife and I cannot begin to think about what Job went through, but we can identify with having something precious being taken suddenly from us. Candace and I still sit down and wonder how things changed so abruptly. However, when we think about this, we can't help but be reminded of all the things we did with Layke for the last time. If you're a parent I would encourage you to treat opportunities you have with your children or family as if they might be your last. While it is impossible to know when the last time may be, Candace and I can look back and see God's thumbprint through it all, and realize how gracious he was to afford us some last opportunities with Layke.

I think of a statement a friend of my family said to me soon after Layke was born and we discovered he was going to face some challenges in life. She said, "I love in the Bible when it says, God went before them," speaking of the children of Israel being brought out of Egypt and journeying through the wilderness. She went on to say that, "God has already gone before us in whatever we are going through." As we look at the last month of Layke's life we are able to see all the gracious opportunities God afforded us. We also recognize that God gave us some special experiences, and proved that He had already gone before us.

I remember when the pandemic had just begun and workplaces shut down and people were forced to stay home. This created many opportunities with their families they never had before, and most likely will never have again. During my time off from work, I worked some at the funeral home where my father-in-law is the funeral director. I remember I was working a graveside funeral and I was standing out in the cemetery of a local church. As I stood there, two rows up was a grave marker for an infant child. A fear came over me and the only thing I could think about was me contracting the virus and taking it home to Layke, for we feared that if he caught it, he would not be able to pull through. After that funeral I told my father-in-law it may be better if I wait 'til the pandemic is over, out of concern for Layke.

In the beginning everyone thought that if you caught the COVID-19 virus your chances of dying were very significant. However, several months passed and the fear of the virus lessened. At the end of September of 2020 Candace and I came down with COVID-19. I never would have thought catching COVID would be a blessing, but in our particular case it was. Candace and I both caught the virus almost a month before Layke died. For two weeks we were instructed to quarantine, meaning we couldn't go anywhere beyond our home, and no one could come around us. It seemed as though our lives had been in such a rush, running here and there. However, when we came down with COVID we were forced to slow down. Thankfully, our symptoms were mild and it was almost like a two-week family vacation spent at home. During this period we were able to enjoy quality time with our children and one another. Many days we would ride the *side-by-side* (Polaris RZR four-wheeler), watch the sunset at the cabin behind our home, and enjoy the slower things of life. As we reflect on this time, we realize God was giving us personal time with our son Layke we would have missed out on, had He not placed these circumstances in our lives. These were precious days given to my family, and we are forever grateful for those memories.

Exactly a week before our son died, Candace, I, and Layke were attending his one-year checkup appointment with his genetic doctor. We had become very acquainted with Dr. Jewett and the genetic team at Brenner Children's Hospital over the course of Layke's life. As I think upon this last doctor's appointment, I remember that Candace was always on the phone with doctors and nurses throughout Layke's life, he continuously had upcoming doctor's appointments. If you never have had to do this, my wife can testify that this is a full-time job keeping up with everything. Layke couldn't have been given a better mother, one who was willing to put all the time and effort into keeping up with all his scheduled appointments.

As difficult as it was at times, I know my wife wishes she could be doing it still. However, during this last appointment we sat there and showed her how strong he had gotten and the progress he was making concerning his weight bearing and prop sitting, which he could do for longer periods than before. Dr. Jewett was so encouraging by telling us how well he was doing and she praised Candace, for she could tell she had been working with him daily on his therapies. It was just such an uplifting doctor's appointment. We also discussed his standing machine he had just been fitted for that was to help him learn what it felt like to stand. This machine was on order and Candace and I were looking forward to getting this machine, because we were hopeful this would increase his chances of being able to stand independently and one day walk, due to the strength it would build in his legs. I remember how good it felt after this appointment. We sat through so many that were discouraging and didn't give a sense of hope, but thankfully this one was different.

In the middle of October, a couple weeks before Layke died, we took the kids to the Alpha and Omega Corn Maze. We asked some other people to go but no one was able to, so it was just going to be Candace, me, Liam, and Layke. Looking back, I'm so thankful the Lord gave us those memories as a family. They had a big trough full of shelled corn and the kids played in it like a sand box. We never wanted Layke to be left out of anything so we put him in there and held him up as he ran his little hands through the corn. Some of the pictures from there are some of my favorites of Layke. I never dreamed that trip would be the last time we would go do something as a family.

Please don't take for granted the opportunities God gives to do something with your children.

Other than to the hospital and to doctor's appointments, the first place Layke went to in this life, was to church. Church was also the last place Layke would go. I would say that Layke went to church more than he went anywhere else. We went to our weekly Tuesday night service and our pastor was preaching revival somewhere that week, so I was in charge of conducting the service. There were two things that stood out to me about this last trip to the House of God: First, Candace took a couple of pictures of Layke there, after church in the pew, and seeing him smile and laugh was very heart-touching. And second was the sermon I preached. Several months prior I began a series of messages on "How Christ Works in Hopeless Situations." I began at the end of Mark chapter 4, in how Christ calmed the storm, then moved to Mark chapter 5, and studied the Maniac of Gadara from whom Jesus cast out all the demons. Then we looked at the woman who had an issue of blood for twelve years until she reached out and touched the hem of His garment, and was healed. Then lastly, that Tuesday night I preached on Jairus. We all know the story of Jairus, he had a daughter who laid sick at the point of death and he ran to Jesus. As they are journeying to Jairus' house Jesus stops to heal the woman with the issue of blood. As they start their journey back, word comes to Jairus that his daughter has died. We know the story Jesus tells Jairus,

"Be not afraid, only believe."

—Mark 5:36c KJV

Although I will say more later, this story and message is what I continually thought about a week later when we found ourselves in a very similar situation that Jairus was in. Little did we know that the next time we would all be in church together would be a week and a half later at his funeral. I would challenge every parent: "Don't take for granted the opportunities you have to take your family to the House of God." I still to this day think while we are in church how I wish I could carry him into the House of God again, and hold him and kiss the back of his head as I used to.

If anyone knows my wife, they know she loves pictures. It seemed like we fussed and fought more when we were trying to go somewhere, because she loved getting pictures and I hated them. If I said it one time I said a hundred times, "We don't have to get a picture every time we go somewhere." However, I've learned to appreciate the fact that my wife took all the pictures she did, because those pictures hold memories I had already forgotten in the short time we had Layke. Every time I look at those last pictures she took of Layke the day before we took him to the hospital, it reminds me that God cares about our desires personally. My wife loves pictures and she talked for at least a month about how excited she was about our kids' Halloween costumes. Liam was dressing up as a bear, and Layke was going to be a lion. On Friday October 30th, the day before Halloween, my wife thought it would be a good idea to put the kids in their Halloween costumes for pictures. This would take some of the stress off of her the next day while we would be trying to get the kids to our families to trick or treat. I've heard her say so many times since Layke has passed that her putting the kids in their costumes the day prior is something so out of the ordinary that she didn't know why she thought to do that. It could have been because she didn't want to hear me complaining about it, I'm not sure, but she did it.

Little did she know that the kids wouldn't get to wear those costumes out that year because the next morning on Halloween we would be taking Layke to the hospital. As I look back on this situation, the Lord knew how much pictures meant to my wife. He knew how excited she was to see the kids in their costumes and He worked it out that she would have that memory forever. I've heard my wife say how God proved how much he cares about even the smallest desires of our heart through that circumstance. Every time I look at those pictures of our children, I see the Lord's thumbprint on the situation. As much as I hated getting pictures, I sure wish I could get one more with Layke.

We got up that Saturday morning as we did many times. We knew that Layke wasn't feeling the greatest because he was teething and we had been at Candace's parent's house the night before carving pumpkins. Layke slept a good bit of the time while Candace's dad held him. This was not unusual for Layke to get like this. Anytime he would run a fever he would become drowsy. He had received some shots earlier that week and he was teething so we were not really alarmed that he was running low-grade fevers and was really tired, because that was how Layke responded to fevers many times prior. However, we got up and we always read the Bible and prayed on Saturday mornings. I can't remember where we read from, but I do remember Candace trying to feed him his bottle with Tylenol in it to diminish the fever he was fighting. After we finished reading she told me, "Maybe we should take him on to the hospital because I don't feel comfortable waiting around for him to get worse."

Layke was showing all the same signs he would show if he was developing pneumonia as he had many times prior, and we thought we would be proactive by taking him on to be examined. Little did I know that would be the last time we would read the

Bible as a family with Layke. Reading the Bible together was something we tried to make a priority. We were privileged to read with Layke when he arrived home from the hospital at his birth, but also do this with him one last time prior to his death.

We still read and pray nightly with Liam and we will often ask him, "Who did we used to read with?"

Sweetly he will say, "Brudder."

To keep track of where we stop and start in our reading, a bookmark with Layke's picture keeps our place. We decided we would continue reading through the entire Bible together as a family and every time we do it, we think of Layke because he was who we started it with. There are so many times I wish I could read and pray with Layke again. The privilege to be able to read and pray with your children is a wonderful memory to have, and we wouldn't trade those memories for anything.

So, after we finished reading that Saturday morning, we took Layke on to the Emergency Room at Brenner's Children's Hospital. We packed just a few things for him in his diaper bag, for we didn't plan to stay. I can still see him laying on our bed asleep as we were getting ready. He slept in his bassinet beside our bed every night, but in the morning after I left for work, Candace often put him in the bed with her and Liam. She would send me pictures of the boys sleeping in the bed or lying there all cuddled up together. Neither of us would have ever dreamed that as we pulled out of the driveway that morning, Layke would not be pulling back in with us. We were faced with the reality David was, when his child died. David understood he couldn't bring that child back, but he could at some point go to where that child now was. That is our consolation now, knowing that even though Layke can't come back to our home, we can go to his new home when God calls us there.

We didn't realize how precious it was to have such a gift in our home, until that gift was no longer there. Even though we can't go back, it does cause us to cherish the time even more that we have our children within our home. There have been many times since Layke went home to be with the Lord that Candace and I both sit thinking about how much we miss Layke being in our home, at which times Liam has often come up and asked, "Why are you crying?"

"Because we miss your brother," I tell him.

In those times I always give Liam a big hug and tell him how much I love him, because if my children don't know anything else, I do want them to know how much we love them and how thankful we are that God gave us the children he did. Even though Layke isn't in our home, he is still in our hearts and every time we gather and pray at the brick fireplace, we always thank God for Liam, and we thank God that He gave us Layke. Having your children in your home is truly a precious gift.

A Sunday School teacher sent me a text after our first child Liam was born and he told me, "Always cherish the times of holding your children while they are a baby." That has always stuck with me, and carries even more meaning now. I remember the Monday before we went to the hospital. I came home from work that evening and I knew I had a little more preparation I needed to get finished to preach on that Tuesday night for our midweek service. I had been studying Jairus and his daughter as mentioned earlier in this chapter. I remember walking through the living room headed toward my study and I walked by Layke in his exersaucer and it was like the Lord spoke to my heart and said, *You better go hold him, because you won't always be able to.* It wasn't an audible voice, but those words ran through my head. I really thought the Lord was telling me one day Layke would get too big and I wouldn't be able to hold him. So I went over there and held him for a few moments and put him back in the exersaucer, then proceeded to my study.

If I would have known then what I do now, I would have held him and not put him down at all. When I think of that instance my mind always runs to the last time I did hold Layke. It was the Sunday afternoon before he died. We were at the hospital and Candace was taking a much-needed nap. I remember saying to myself, *I don't have anything I need to do, and no where I need to be and I'm going to enjoy holding Layke.* So I got him out of the bed and adjusted his IV and oxygen tubes so they wouldn't be in the way, and we sat in that reclining chair in the room for a couple of hours. Layke fell asleep there in my arms that day. Typically when Layke fell asleep with me holding him, I found a way to transfer him to his basinet or to the crib, but this day I just held him there in my arms. Little did I know that it would be the last time I would hold him. What bothers me so much about that is when I got to the hospital that Monday they were moving Layke from the intermediate care unit to the intensive care unit. That evening prior Layke had been fussy and irritable and I was scared that if I picked him up to hold him it would arouse him and he would be fussy, so I avoided irritating him. I thought it would be best if he rested.

However, my wife did hold him that evening. It was only an hour or so before we heard the devastating news from the ICU doctor, that my wife held our darling son. Layke during that time was somewhat uncomfortable and unsettled and my wife knew he may need repositioning. She lifted him from his bed and held him there in the reclining chair. He immediately seemed more comfortable as she held him. Candace seemed to have a special touch in calming him down when he was unsettled. Many times when no one else could give him comfort, she could, and it was no different during this time. She gently rested his head against her shoulder, and wrapped her arms around his little body. I saw her kiss the top of his head as she said, "Shh . . . Mommy loves you."

Those were the last times we held our son, except when we got to hold him while they took him off life support. I write this with tears in my eyes. There truly do come last times in this life. If you are a parent there will come a last time you get to hold your children. It may not be due to death, it could slip right on by with age as they get bigger and lose interest in being held. However I would challenge any parent to cherish the moments and opportunities God gives during this life, because there do come last times here on Earth, and they truly are gifts from God.

TAYLOR & CANDACE MILLER

Chapter 8:

The Bereaving
of This Gift

"The Lord gave, and the Lord hath taken away;
blessed be the name of the Lord"

—Job 1:21b

I AM REMINDED of what I heard a pastor state in a sermon from Job chapter 1. He brought out two points that are very true and impactful. In the first verse of chapter 1 in the Book of Job the Bible says,

"There was a man."
—Job 1:1a KJV

Then in verse number 6 the Bible says,

"Now there was day."

—Job 1:6a KJV

On that day Job lost his wealth, his health, and even his ten children. Things happened to Job that day he never thought imaginable. The truth is that for a believer, and even if one is an unbeliever, life will bring a day when it seems like the bottom is falling out from beneath us, a day when life delivers a blow it seems you may never recover from, a day that changes your life forever. I would never put my character or my trial on the same level as Job's. However, there was a day we felt like the bottom had fallen out, a day that so blindsided my family we were in no way prepared for it. That moment came for us at midnight between November 2nd and 3rd of 2020. This was a day that will never be forgotten in our lives, for it is a day that crosses our minds every day in some form or fashion.

Candace noticed that Friday Layke was somewhat feverish and lethargic. However, he was teething and had vaccinations a few days prior. Both of these can result in children running fevers. Candace had been treating him with fever reducing medication throughout the day. When we got up that Saturday morning Layke was still running a fever and still acting very drowsy. He was beginning to sound a little congested in his chest, which is the way he would present each time he was developing pneumonia. Layke had dealt with many recurrent diagnoses of pneumonia and infections throughout his life, we knew what signs and symptoms were typical for him to develop in the beginning stages of his sickness. Early that morning, we got up and read our daily Bible reading as Candace fed him his bottle with medication in it. During that time, she noticed Layke wasn't drinking well and wasn't alert enough to safely swallow the milk without aspirating. When we finished reading, Candace told me we should take him to be evaluated at the hospital before his symptoms became worse. Layke's genetic doctor told us from his birth that Layke would need to be treated more aggressively than a normal child, due to his immune system being compromised. My wife and I agreed the best thing to do was to take Layke on to the emergency room.

Thirteen Hours in the ER

That Saturday on Halloween morning, we pulled out of our driveway and headed toward Brenner Children's Hospital Emergency Room. Little did we know we were also headed into a storm like we had never imagined. As mentioned earlier in the book, we had no idea when we left that morning we would not be bringing Layke back with us. We weren't even completely convinced he would be admitted and have to stay overnight. As before, our assumption was that they would perform an x-ray, tell us he was developing a little bit of pneumonia, and treat him with antibiotics he could take at home. We had been through this enough that it had almost become routine. We didn't pack clothes, we just took Layke and his diaper bag and went on our way.

As we got to the ER we did what we had done many times in the past. We pulled up, gave our keys to the valet parker, and went inside to check in. They took us back with nearly no wait at all, and soon had us settled in a room. As the nurses and doctors came in and assessed Layke, they began asking the normal questions. As their assessment continued, the question came up, "Have either of you been exposed to COVID-19 recently?"

"We both had COVID-19 less than a month prior," we replied, and we noticed concerns began to rise. More nurses began coming in, more tests were being ordered, and labs were being drawn.

Then they explained, "There is an inflammatory response seen to develop in children weeks after being exposed to COVID-19. We generally see this response within three to four weeks after exposure."

Layke fell right into that time frame.

They continued, "This response is called MIS-C, which stands for *multisystem inflammatory syndrome in children*. This is a very new syndrome, and not widely known." Very little information was given, due to its uniqueness. "Layke is presenting a lot of the physical signs of this very diagnosis, so we'd like to work him up for these tests."

In return, I began to do what all medical professionals would not advise—research the internet to get a more in-depth explanation on what this was. As I was reading, I felt my stomach turn within me and my heart sink. My lip quivered as I told Candace to read what I read. The internet said it was very serious in children and could be fatal. We both became very concerned and began asking questions as the healthcare team was in and out of his room.

"We haven't seen a child yet with this response," they said, "and all we are doing is trying to rule it out while coming up with a definitive diagnosis for him."

We were getting very nervous because we felt like this was way more serious than we thought. Many blood draws, scans, and hours of waiting went by. One of the medical professionals came back into the room, looked at her computer, and pulled up a chart, hoping lab results were ready. With relief in her voice she said, "He has *rhinovirus!*"

Of course, you never want to hear your child has a virus, but they felt the symptoms he was presenting were from the rhinovirus and not MISC, which seemed to be a much better alternative.

"We haven't completely ruled out MISC just yet, but we're fairly confident most of what we are seeing is coming from the rhinovirus, which is something that stems from a common cold."

More results came in, and the majority of them came back normal, which led them to believe Layke did not have the MISC. This was a major relief for us, given the survival rate and chance of recovery from a virus such as this was very good.

They continued monitoring his oxygen, because at times it dropped lower than it should have. Soon they placed him on a small amount of oxygen through a nasal cannula to assist with his breathing. It was still very apparent Layke was lethargic, and he was sleeping for the majority of the time we spent in the emergency room. Every now and then he would arouse, make eye contact with those big blue eyes, then quickly drift back off to sleep. The fact that he hadn't been more alert, even after getting his fever under control, was a bit concerning. The emergency room team decided to order a CT of his head, to make sure everything looked okay. As the results came back and looked fairly good, they were concerned as to why he continued to sleep. One of the doctors came in and suggested they perform a spinal tap to rule out meningitis. Soon after the spinal tap was completed, those results came back normal as well. We had now been in the ER for thirteen hours, and they decided to admit him, especially since he was dependent on oxygen at this point. Before moving us to a hospital room, they explained that after a day or so he should recover from the virus, and be back to his normal self.

Candace stayed the night with him, as I left around midnight to head home and gather the needed supplies to stay for the next few nights before bringing Layke back home. Little did we know the thirteen hours we had in the ER were a blessing in disguise because we were able to spend that entire day just with Layke. Our attention was solely focused on him, and holding our child. During that time, we took pictures with him and spent quality time with him, looking for the best care and treatment possible for our son. Of course, we would've never chosen this place or this setting, however, it was still cherished quality time when we look back. We are forever grateful to God for that precious one-on-one time with Layke.

Our Last Day Together

I returned to the hospital that next morning around 8:30 a.m. for the doctors to round. As they came by his room and completed their assessment there was nothing alarming to report. They were just keeping a watch on his oxygen and wanting to wean him down to room air as he could tolerate. What I didn't realize was this was going to be the last day I would spend with my son before the bottom fell out, so to speak. As mentioned earlier in this book, that afternoon would be the last time I would hold him. If I would have known what I know now, I don't think I would have ever put him down. I held him that day, as he slept in my arms.

For the most part it appeared to be somewhat of a calm day there in the hospital. He ran a fever, and the nurses kept a close eye on his oxygen while reducing his fever with medication. He seemed to be doing pretty well, and nothing alarming was taking place. Candace and I hadn't eaten lunch, and it was close to four o'clock that afternoon. We decided to leave quickly to grab something to eat. Layke was sleeping peacefully, and the nurse encouraged us to leave as she assured us she would keep a close eye on him. As we returned to eat at his bedside, we buzzed the nurses' station to let us in. After giving them our room number and the correct passcode, we begin walking towards Layke's room. As we walked by the nurses' station, one of the nurses asked, "You both are the parents in room 16, correct?"

"Yes we are."

"We want to let you know there are a lot of people in there."

We took off running to his room, as fear and anxiety came over us. Sure enough, the room was filled with doctors and nurses surrounding his bed. Quickly, the nurse came to us and informed us they had to call a rapid response. She continued to say that his oxygen kept dropping, and she couldn't get him to arouse. Thankfully, by the time we got there his oxygen had risen to a safe percentage. They discussed what the best move was from here, and from that point on decided to move him into the step-down unit called the *intermediate care unit*. This was a higher level of nursing care compared to what he was currently receiving. It fell in-between the normal pediatric floor and the intensive care unit (ICU). This transition would provide the needed medical attention, if he would happen to continue with this desaturation in his oxygen. Therefore, his medical team felt this was the best move, and we as his parents completely agreed.

My wife and I had no clue what was coming, but I remember telling Candace I did not have a good feeling. However, I never imagined what was around the bend. I was becoming concerned for Layke more than ever. As we moved down to the intermediate care unit, we were greeted by a couple of nurses who would be giving Layke a lot of attention. They were naming various tests that they would be performing, and assured us he would be very closely monitored while he was there. The doctor who would be caring for Layke also came by to visit. We had many questions, unsure of why our son's fevers seemed to be out of control even with medication around the clock, and why his oxygen continued to plummet. My wife was questioning whether his doctors had overlooked something, and whether we should get the infectious disease specialist involved at this point.

This series of events was very alarming, especially since most viruses, and in particular the rhinovirus, wouldn't seem to have such detrimental effects. We watched our child suffer through many rounds of double pneumonia with breathing difficulties, fevers, aspiration, etc., but this seemed to be raising a fear in us more than anything he had ever faced. After expressing our concern and confusion, the doctor explained he felt that Layke was at the peak of the virus, and that these symptoms weren't necessarily abnormal for his diagnosis. He went on to explain that every child responds differently, but they felt strongly that the rhinovirus was the only issue here. It was reassuring to us that they would be keeping a closer watch on him now. I stayed by his bedside until 10:30 p.m. that night, and headed back home because I was going to attempt going to work the next morning. At that point in time, I had in my mind that I should work as much as I possibly could so I would be able to be off when it was really needed or if things escalated with Layke's situation. However, little did I know, these were the days and moments I needed to be with him more than ever.

The Longest Day of our Lives

I went to work that next morning. Looking back, this was a day that would feel as if it would never end. It truly was the longest day we have ever had. One day would run into another, and we were left wondering how two days had come and gone. It seemed like one never ending day for the both of us.

Candace sent me pictures of Layke that morning after his first night in the step down ICU. One of them was of Layke lying in the bed and he was smiling. He had a fan at the bedside blowing on his blonde hair, trying to cool down his temperature. Then she sent me another picture around 10 a.m. that morning. He was sitting up in a highchair getting ready to eat there in his room.

This was the best he had looked in my opinion. He was wide awake, and just looked so good sitting upright. I thought to myself, *He will be coming home in a day or so for sure.* We felt like he was turning the corner.

That day at work I remember telling my boss and a close friend I work with that Layke was in the hospital. I told them he was doing pretty good, but if something changed, I may have to leave. As the day went on, Candace told me they were having to boost his oxygen some throughout the day. She sent me a video of him and you could see him retracting somewhat in his chest and abdomen while he was breathing. This was a classic sign that he was struggling and was in distress. As I watched the video, my heart broke for him. I could see him struggling to breathe, and my desire was to be there with him. So that afternoon I spoke with my boss about leaving work a little early and headed towards the hospital.

As soon as I pulled out of work, Candace called and told me that they had made the decision to move Layke to the PICU, which stands for the *pediatric intensive care unit.* His oxygen continued to drop as the day progressed, increasing his need for more supplemental oxygen. He had maxed out on the amount they could safely administer there in the step down unit, and his blood pressure was dropping for unknown reasons. His medical team indicated that he would be the least sick child in the ICU, but felt that since they had a room available he would get the best care there, and the most attention. However, when Candace relayed this news to me, I remember getting very fearful. I called two of my close pastor friends, along with my pastor to inform them of what was going on. They assured me they would be praying for him, as I voiced how concerned we were for our child. It appeared that slowly, he was trickling down hill, instead of making improvements like we had expected.

As I arrived to his room, the medical team was in the process of moving him, wheeling the bed out of the room as I walked through the double doors. The hospital staff wheeled him down the hall to the PICU. Candace and I walked behind him holding hands, as we took several deep breaths. Upon reaching the room they were placing him in, we noticed how big and well-lit it was. As nurses began to settle Layke into his new room, the doctor was giving a report to the oncoming physician because it was right before shift change that we were transferred. After their reports finished, the doctor that would be taking over his care for the night came in and talked to us personally.

He explained that many people hear of rhinovirus and think it is just a common cold, and he stated in most cases, it is. He went on to explain that the only rhinovirus cases they see in the PICU are the most severe. He also explained the course and pattern they generally see with this virus. He said they see children really peak with the symptoms of this virus around day three or four, but after that they tend to see children make a turn around and recover. He said that everything he saw with Layke indicated he was on that very same path. He informed us their goal was to support him until he made the turnaround, and then they would get him back to the regular floor.

After that conversation with the doctor, it was as if a load had been lifted off of us. We had been concerned because we saw him slowly getting worse instead of better. When he told us this, trusting he had experienced this pattern many times with various children, we felt sure Layke was on the path of improving soon, he just needed to get over this bump in the road. We informed our family of what the doctor had told us, and spent that evening in the hospital by our son's side.

It seemed as though Layke was irritable that entire evening, and that if he wasn't sleeping he would get fussy. Candace and I tried to calm him any way we possibly could. We tried simple things such as singing to him, and showing him one of his favorite light up toys to take his mind off of all the struggle. My wife also worked closely with the nurse, administering his medications and trying to reposition him to make him most comfortable. The last thing I wanted to do was to arouse him and get him upset. So that evening, I did not hold him at all. I stood over his bed many times, but never held him for fear I would cause him to become more upset. Candace held him next to his bed in the reclining chair, at one point following an episode of Layke becoming very upset. She told me she just felt like he needed to change positions and get out of that bed.

She held him upright in her lap for a moment and he was okay, but it wasn't long before we realized he couldn't seem to get comfortable no matter what we or the medical team seemed to do. Looking back, we know why he couldn't get settled. In those moments, our son was fighting for his life, and we didn't even realize it. It was the night prior to the presidential election so I had the TV on and was watching the news. To this day, I haven't been able to really watch the news, because I should've had all my attention focused on Layke that night. I feel very guilty for taking attention off of him, and placing it elsewhere.

Periodically that evening, the monitor went off and the nurse came in to adjust his pulse oximeter. Layke's oxygen bounced up and down, and his blood pressure was low, as they were treating this by administering fluids through an IV given over a very quick period of time. Each time the nurses heard his monitor go off, they immediately came running. They were paying very close attention to him, despite the fact everyone felt like he was going to be making the turnaround.

It was closing in on 11 o'clock that night, and since I thought Layke was going to be improving soon, I figured I would try to go to work again the next day. The doctors were making their rounds once again, and I decided to stay, to be there as they talked about their plan for Layke. Unfortunately, Layke was their last room for report that night, as his room was at the very end of the unit. I waited until midnight and they exited his room to give an overview of his plan of care. Candace and I stepped out into the hallway to listen in to the report, and they encouraged us to be a part. The same doctor who gave us the positive report earlier was giving this report as well. He told his staff his goal for the remainder of the night was to wean the oxygen down, and do some chest physical therapy to loosen the secretions, which would help with the congestion. Also, he said he would like to see him back up on the normal floor within the next day.

He was very optimistic, and hopeful the staff could get him safely out of this distress. After hearing another positive report, my heart was very encouraged and at peace with the direction Layke was headed in. I went to Layke's bedside and gave him a kiss on the head, and told him goodbye. I hugged my wife as well, and asked her to call me if anything changed throughout the night.

A very gracious lady from our church offered up her home that was twenty minutes away from the hospital. She was staying with her mother during this time, so her home was vacant. She knew that we lived well over an hour away from the hospital, and it was a challenging drive. My plan was to go to her house and spend the night, allowing me to get more rest than if I were to drive all the way back to our home. I remember pulling into the lady's home, and I had just unlocked the door when Candace called me. I could hear the fear in her voice when she told me that she didn't know where I was, but I needed to come back. I was startled because we had such a positive report just maybe twenty minutes prior, and the last thing I was anticipating was a call like that.

She then FaceTimed me so I could see the room and what was taking place. I saw a room full of nurses, and the doctor who had just given us such a positive report. All of the sudden, I heard that same doctor turn to my wife and say, "Ma'am there is a lot that I cannot understand. I'm going to have to take control of the situation. We are going to go ahead and put him on the ventilator. I'm going to have to ask you to step out of the room."

Those words fell on my heart like a load of bricks. I immediately told Candace I was on my way. I picked up my bag, locked the door, and started back to the hospital. I called my family and my pastor and informed them of what was going on. I prayed the entire way there, asking, "God have mercy on my son." I was very fearful, thinking of this happening while during the COVID pandemic, it seemed once someone went on the ventilator, they did not come off. I was terrified that would be the fate of my son.

As I parked in the parking deck, I ran to the elevator and started up to the sixth floor of the hospital. I got off the elevator and looked to my right. I saw my wife sitting in the waiting room with one of the nurses we knew personally. She had her face in her hands crying while that nurse had her arm around her. I went in and we sat there and wept together in the waiting room, fearful of what was going to be the outcome. We were scared Layke would become dependent on the ventilator, and not be able to come off. We knelt there in that waiting room, and began praying that God would have mercy on Layke.

The nurse informed us he was very sick. We desperately wanted to get back to him. As we sat there in the waiting room, it was just the nurse, my wife, and me. We heard the door open and it was the doctor. He called us back to a private waiting room to talk. We sat down and he began to go over Layke's current situation. He informed us Layke was very sick, and his situation was very dynamic. He told us he needed to insert some arterial lines to help maintain his blood pressure and monitor it safely, due to it dropping to a dangerous range. He also said there was some bleeding as they intubated him, and once they inserted the intubation tube, he was able to see that Layke was much sicker than they originally thought.

As we sat there listening intently, he received a phone call. I was very frightened. "I'll be right there," the doctor said and hung up. the phone. He told us he had to go, and immediately got up and left the room. A few moments passed and the door swung open again. It was this same doctor telling us he needed to begin the process of inserting the arterial lines.

"Please, do whatever needs to be done," we said.

I called a close pastor friend of mine who I knew wouldn't mind me calling in the middle of the night. I told him what was going on, and I really desired his prayers for my son. He assured me he would be praying. At this time, we were walking into the valley of the shadow of death.

As we sat in the small private waiting area, my wife took a call from a friend who heard about Layke's situation. She was interrupted by the door opening abruptly. The doctor rushed in to deliver the most awful words I have ever heard spoken.

"Your son's heart has stopped, and we are doing CPR," he said.

As those words fell on our ears, Candace fell to the floor so desperate, crying out to God, "My baby, my baby. Why God? Why?"

I immediately fell down with her there on the waiting room floor, trying to hold her, and do whatever I could to comfort her. I remember those hopeless screams—even though they were right there, they sounded like they were miles and miles away. I remember thinking to myself, *All the therapies, all the sleepless nights in the hospital, all the doctor's visits, and all the time my wife invested in our son, it's all over,* not to mention she carried this child in her womb for nine months, and delivered our precious son into this world. The bond between a mother and her child I know is indescribable. I watched her love pour out for him since the day he was born, and I knew how strong my love was for him as his father.

My heart ached like never before, shattered into a million pieces. The work we hoped would one day result in a healthy child, ended in death. We laid there on the floor weeping for what seemed like an eternity. We got up slowly to see that very doctor standing there in respect for us. He and the nurse expressed how sorry they were, and that they were still doing CPR.

My wife called her family and her dad answered the phone. She started crying, "Daddy, Daddy, his heart stopped."

I was heartbroken as my wife delivered these words to her family. I couldn't begin to imagine what my wife was going through at that moment. It was simply devastating. My wife and I began to embrace one another and wept together there in that lonely waiting room. Candace told me she needed to escape from that small room for a moment, so we walked out into the main PICU waiting area, which was a larger room and was completely free of any other families. There in that room, we held hands, and I wrapped my wife tightly in my arms as we paced that waiting area for what seemed like an eternity. Walking from one end of the room to the other we prayed and cried, wondering how we ended up in this devastating situation.

Suddenly, one of the nurses came running into the room and said, "We have a pulse!" My wife and I started rejoicing and thanking the Lord for this news. The nurse said 30 minutes passed between his heart stopping and the time they were able to regain a heartbeat. This was immediately worrisome to my wife and I, as we thought about all of the long-term complications and injuries this can cause to one's body when blood flow is compromised for that length of time. Shortly thereafter, the doctor reentered the room and explained that because Layke was not responding well to the ventilator, they would be moving him to the highest form of life support called *extracorporeal membrane oxygenation* (ECMO).

This machine functions as one's heart and lungs. All the blood from one's body is run out into a machine that puts oxygen in the blood, then pumps it back into the body. We were not familiar with this machine, and it seemed very scary that our child was dependent on something such as this. The doctor explained this would be "heroic," but it was what they had to do to potentially save his life. At that point, we were scared that Layke was getting so far gone that he would never recover, but whatever measures it took, we wanted the life of our son.

My wife and I wanted so badly to be with Layke at that time. We felt so helpless, and desired nothing more than to have our little Layke back with us as he was before. We proceeded back out to the normal waiting room, when soon another nurse came through the door and said, "His heart has stopped again, and we are doing CPR."

Our hearts sank with sorrow again. I thought to myself, *Why is this happening?* I didn't understand how we could be brought to the lowest point of despair thinking our son was dead, then rejoicing because he was alive, and now back to the bottom thinking he is gone again. My wife and I continued walking up and down the waiting room holding hands, praying, begging God for mercy again. I cannot begin to describe the roller coaster of emotions we felt in those hours. At that point, I was scared of that door that led back to the patient rooms. We didn't know what news would be brought to us after that door swung open. It was a time of such pain and anxiety.

This was a situation we never dreamed we would be in. I felt a lot like David did when he said,

> "My heart is severely pained within me, And the terrors of death are fallen upon me. Fearfulness and trembling are come upon me, and horror hath overwhelmed me. And I said, Oh that I had wings like a dove! For then would I fly away, and be at rest."
>
> —Psalms 55:4-6 KJV

This is how we felt during these moments. If I could, I would have gathered up Layke and my family and taken us out of this situation. But I couldn't. I couldn't do anything. It was such a helpless place. We were there in that lonely waiting room with no one around and scared like we had never been before. Though we didn't realize it then, there was someone in there with us, and He was there before we got there. It was God Himself. We felt alone, but I am grateful for the child of God. We are never alone and when it seems He is nowhere around, that's when He is closest by. He was walking the waiting room floors alongside of us holding our hands during this time.

My mind went back to the message I preached that previous Tuesday night on Jairus and his daughter. One of my main points in that message was "A Devastating Report." For the bible says,

> "While he yet spake, there came from the ruler of the synagogue's house certain which said, Thy daughter is dead: why troublest the Master and further."
>
> —Mark 5:35 KJV

I couldn't help but think of what Jesus said to Jairus at that point. He said,

> "Be not afraid, only believe."
> —Mark 5:36 KJV

It was easier for me to try to think about that story than to think on the situation we were currently in. Every time I thought about the reality we were facing, my heart ached and cringed, so I just kept thinking and praying that Scripture. We were begging God to work a miracle. We were calling others and asking them to pray. It was in the middle of the night and I wasn't hesitant to call, because that was my son fighting for his life, and I was willing to call or ask anyone I knew to pray for him.

Suddenly, I heard the door open again, scared for what they were going to tell us. One of the nurses said, "We have a pulse."

We began rejoicing again, thanking God for answering prayer. They told us they were indeed going to put him on *extracorporeal membrane oxygenation* (ECMO), as discussed, which would require surgery. They informed us the surgeon had arrived, but before they could perform the surgery we would have to sign a consent form. The surgeon came over and spoke to us, explaining the procedure he would shortly perform. After he finished, I asked him if I could have a word of prayer with him. If there was ever a time I wanted God to be with someone, it was then. After we got done praying we were told we could go kiss him before they began the surgery.

As we anxiously walked back through the doors, leading to where our precious son laid, we noticed he wasn't moving at all. We immediately noticed the bruises from where they had to perform CPR. He felt cool to the touch, and his little body already seemed swollen from the trauma he had endured. It was heart-wrenching, as it seemed he was already gone. Candace and I both talk about how we still can see him lying there on that operating table. It was like something you see in a dream. Unfortunately, it was a reality to us. We leaned down and kissed those chubby cheeks we had loved on so many times before. I, being a pastor, had prayed many times with people before they went to surgery. The very least I could do for my son was pray for him. So, my wife and I prayed with our dear son, standing over him, begging God one more time for mercy.

We walked out and they began surgery. In the waiting room, our families started to arrive. Thankfully, the hospital allowed our families to be with us for a limited time, even during the COVID-

19 pandemic. The waiting room filled with our family members, our pastor, and his family.

After about an hour or so, the doctors came out and explained the surgery was complete. They began to go over the situation with us. They told us things that made us hopeful, but also presented the facts and the severity of the situation. However, we knew that for our son to pull through, it would take a miracle from God, and that is what we prayed for.

I remember at this point it was a struggle to even stand. I felt like my legs would give way any second. It took a conscious effort to pick my feet up and take a step. It had been over 24 hours since my wife and I had slept. I had heard many people use the old saying, "It was hard to put one foot in front of the other." That day I knew exactly what that felt like. This no doubt was the longest night of our lives.

One of the nurses came and told us they had him on ECMO now and we were welcome to come see him. However, they warned us before we went back that it was a lot to take in, looking at the machine and someone being hooked up to it. As we laid eyes on him, it was truly hard to come to terms with all that was before us. Looking at our little child on a machine so massive and extravagant, seemed unreal. He lay there as if lifeless. We touched his little body, which seemed so cold. We looked up at the monitor displaying his vital signs to remind us he was still alive. The lady running the ECMO reminded us that this machine was literally his heart and lungs at this time. His little body had lines going from what seemed like every orifice. What a dreaded sight for a parent to behold. However, my wife and I kept thanking the Lord for the simple fact God had granted mercy once again, and that there was some hope for our son.

After spending some time by Layke's bedside and coming to grips with the reality we were in, we had to gather our belongings from the room Layke was in previously. This was the room where we had left our child, not knowing we would leave this room and be told moments later, "His heart has stopped." All of Layke's belongings, as well as ours, were left in this room. This is the room we had planned to spend a night or two in, and quickly see improvements in our son. I remember walking down the hall and approaching the room he once lay in. This was the last place I had made eye contact with my son, kissed him while he was alert, and knew he could hear me say the words, "I love you buddy."

This was the room I had walked out of nearly six hours earlier, encouraged and hopeful Layke would soon be coming home. However, this time as I went back to that room, I was discouraged and fearful we may never take our son home again. The previous six hours were the longest and darkest hours of our lives. I never had a sleepless night like that before. As Candace and I observed the room, it was completely empty in the middle where Layke's bed once was. All that was in the room were our belongings that had been left, and the empty rocking chair my wife held him in hours prior. His diaper bag, our clothes bags, and a couple other items were stacked up in the corner of the room against the window. I asked Candace, "Is this where they would have been doing CPR on him?"

"Yes, it would have been," she said.

You could see empty syringes and gloves thrown across the room, as if a storm had swept right through there. I could envision it in my mind, the doctors and nurses there, working on him, as diligently as they could. I never knew that when I walked out of that room six hours earlier we were getting ready to enter into a storm like this. It was a painful reality, and all I could think was, *God have mercy.*

The Hardest Prayer I ever Prayed

There were several prayers that were prayed during this time. I can remember praying some of them, others I do not recall. There was one in particular I do remember praying, and quite frankly, it was the hardest prayer I have ever prayed. We spent time switching out of Layke's room that day. The policy was that only two people could be back in the room at one time. There were several times throughout that day I uttered prayers asking for a miracle, asking for healing, asking for God to turn this situation around. However, it felt like nothing I prayed was getting through. As many have said, "It felt as if the Heavens were brass."

I came out of Layke's room and allowed Candace's mother to go back. I walked into the waiting room and it was completely empty. As a preacher, I had stated multiple times standing behind the pulpit how important it was to pray according to the will of God. Unfortunately, I did not want to do that because I was terrified of what God's will truly was in this situation. However, me refusing to pray for God's will doesn't change God's will in the least bit, nor does it hinder God's will from being accomplished. Still, I was scared to pray for it. I couldn't come to grips with praying that if it was God's will for Him to take my son on, that it be done. Nevertheless, I felt in my heart that was what God wanted me to pray, for His will to be accomplished.

I remember walking to the far corner of that hospital waiting room, where no one could see me through the windows. I slowly got down on my hands and knees and honestly told God, "I can't even pray for Your will to be done, without You helping me pray for it." In that prayer I told God that it was my desire for Him to heal my son here on this Earth. I realized that if that was not His will, I knew it would not be done. I went on to tell God, "If it is Your will to take my son, please give us the grace to make it through, because without it, it is simply unbearable." I ended the

89

prayer saying the words of our Lord when in the garden He prayed,

"Nevertheless not my will, but thine, be done."
—Luke 22:42 KJV

A Peaceful Calm

As the day went on, we stayed there in Layke's hospital room. There was a little couch beside his bed where we could be close to him. The room continuously stayed well-lit with bright lights overhead due to the ECMO tech sitting behind the machine constantly monitoring it, and making sure it was functioning properly. Candace laid down on the couch as I sat on one end. There was a time or two she allowed herself to doze off for a few minutes. I recall sitting there nervous and anxious about what the outcome of all this would be. The nurses worked very strenuously in that room. It seemed as if they were just back and forth, bringing in new bags of medications, taking blood samples, administering blood products, etc. I remember with every ding the monitor would make my heart jumped, wondering what it meant, fearful it meant something bad.

Then it seemed, as though all of the sudden, there came a calmness in the room. The work of the nurse seemed to let up, and like a sigh of relief, she told us he was weaning off the blood pressure medicine, which was amazing. His organs were responding somewhat. This was the most hopeful we felt in well over twenty-four hours. We sat in next to where he lay so helpless as the time passed. We had no idea how long Layke would be on ECMO, weeks or even longer, so we knew we would have to rest at some point. The technician running the machine came to us and told us that if there ever was a good time to go get some rest, it would be now. We had been given a hotel room nearby, and some of our family was staying there as well. As much as we didn't want to leave his bedside, we decided to go try to get a few hours of sleep, if possible. For it was going on two full days with just a short nap for both of us.

My wife left her contact number with the technician and nurses and asked them to call if anything at all changed in the night. They assured us they would not hesitate to let us know. We kissed Layke goodnight and hesitantly, headed towards the hotel room holding onto some hope. The very fact that he had been weaned off the blood pressure medicine meant that his heart was working with the machine. This was miraculous in our eyes. So we prayed that night kneeling next to that hotel bed, once again begging God for his mercies and grace to be extended to us and our son, then we crawled into bed around midnight.

The Call in the Night

Around 3:00 a.m. we were awoken to the sound of Candace's phone loudly ringing. As she looked at it, she said with anxiety in her voice, "It's the hospital." My heart sank, knowing they would not be calling us at a time such as this unless something was wrong.

The doctor told my wife we needed to come back to the hospital as soon as possible. He explained since we left Layke's heart had quickly grown weaker. We knew what this meant. Unless the Lord intervened, our son wouldn't be here much longer. We frantically got up, grabbed our belongings, and headed to the hospital.

We arrived and went up to the sixth floor, where they informed us Layke had been losing a lot of blood internally, and they were doing all they could to keep up with that loss. They said they could do surgery to try and drain the blood, but due to the blood thinners Layke was on for the ECMO to work properly, the doctor explained Layke most likely would bleed out and die during that process.

"We don't want to do that to our son," Candace said.

She told the doctor she would like to speak with the cardiologist and the neurologist to see what his heart function truly was, as well as his brain function. We were concerned about his organs and his brain function due to the lack of blood flow during the two episodes of his heart stopping, and the length of time CPR was administered. We knew this could cause detrimental effects on the function of the brain and other organs. My wife explained to the doctor she wanted a clear clinical picture of what things looked like for our son. She wanted to hear the hard truth of things, whether it was good or terrible.

A Day Filled With Grace

As this day continued, reality was truly setting in. However, there was something else setting in as well, and that was the grace of God. These days were the hardest days in our lives. On the other side, in these days we experienced the grace of God in a way we had never experienced before. The grace God gave us during these times was a grace tailored and designed just for us to face the harshest reality we had ever known. We noticed that grace in several different ways that day.

We contacted our families who were all staying very close to the hospital, and told them things weren't looking good. The words I remember saying the most that morning when I called our family, pastor, and friends was, "If the Lord doesn't intervene, Layke isn't going to make it." Those were very hard words to say as a parent. It was as if it were a dream as those words flowed from my lips.

That day was very emotional for us, but there was something different about both Candace and me. We were heartbroken, but God gave us grace for that day we hadn't had up until then. That grace calmed our hearts and our minds. That grace gave my wife a clear mind to speak to the doctors and make decisions. I remember thinking, *This is the same mother who was screaming in despair when the doctor told us Layke's heart had stopped, but now she is able to have a clear mind to hear very difficult reports from the doctors, and in return ask very serious and difficult questions.*

The neuro team soon came in and did their exam. After they completed their assessment, they informed us there was no sign of brain function, and told us that if his heart began functioning better and he were to pull through this, he would be on a ventilator with no brain function his entire life. We knew this was not the life we wanted for our son. In addition to learning that devastating news, we soon found from the cardiologist that Layke's heart was extremely weak and declining rapidly.

Grace in Goodbye

We knew it was God alone who had given us grace to say goodbye. There are some things in life that are absolutely unbearable apart from the grace of God. I believe one of those is saying goodbye to one that you love so dear.

After hearing the reports given by the doctors, we knew we were going to have to make the decision to take Layke off life support. There was no question in our minds what the right thing to do was. However, this is a decision no parent ever wants to make, no matter how clear the answer is. I have never witnessed a mother as selfless as Candace was in that moment. After all my wife had invested in him, and how much she loved him, all she wanted was for him to have the best quality of life possible. She knew what was best for our son, and it wasn't keeping him here.

The most hopeless I have ever felt in life was after coming to grips with the fact that Layke wasn't going to make it. I walked over to the corner of the room he lay in and grabbed his diaper bag. I took it to the room where our family was gathered because I knew we would have to get our belongings out shortly. I couldn't help but think of all the times we took that diaper bag with Layke, and everywhere we went with him, but this time, it wouldn't be with him. I walked away with that thought resonating in my heart.

As we were getting ready to make one of the most difficult decisions we have ever made, we were reminded that in the end, it was not our decision to make. Life and death are in the hands of the Lord, not ours. Our pastor made that clear to us when he told us, "The doctors have done all they can do." He told us, "You have done all you can do. Now it is time for the Lord to do His work. When you decide to take Layke off life support, the Lord will choose to take him or leave him. It is not in your hands." Hearing those words was very comforting to us, because we had not seen it in that same light.

It became very evident what we would have to do, as we saw Layke's condition worsening.

Throughout that day we went to his bedside and just wept over him. I told him over and over, "Dadda is so proud of you." I told him how much I loved him. My wife spent countless hours at his bedside. I saw her weep, holding his bruised and swollen hands.

"Mommy loves you so much, Layke," she said, as she kissed his chubby cheeks once again.

There was a song we practiced singing as a family before all of this happened to Layke. The song was entitled, "Tell Me a

Time." We stood there over his bed that day and sang the chorus of that song with tears in our eyes and cracks in our weak voices.

Tell me a time He's not been faithful.
Tell me a morning his mercies weren't new,
tell me a moment that He wasn't able to carry you through.
Tell me a day He was less than almighty,
when he could not roll back the tide.
Child when you look back,
you're gonna find there was never a time.

Those words were never more true than in that moment. The Lord knew that exact song and the encouragement it would be to us, as He knew we would be standing over our son's death bed. Truly, He was still almighty and just as powerful as He had ever been, regardless of the fact that our son was dying. We were witnessing God's will unfold before our eyes, knowing He could work miracles if it was His plan. Our job was to accept and trust the situation the Lord put us in. Candace and I both can testify that God is always faithful, especially in those toughest valleys we walk through.

There were a lot of questions going through my mind after we realized the end was here for Layke's life on Earth. *Why would God give us a child only to take him fourteen months later? How could God do this or allow this to happen to us?* With all those thoughts and questions running through my mind, I remembered studying and preparing a message I preached back around Easter of that year. In my study, I recalled reading a story that I read from Charles Swindoll's book, *From Darkness to Dawn.* In that book there was a story told of a tragic plane crash that happened over the Grand Canyon. There were no survivors in the crash. Days later there was a memorial service held at the Grand Canyon in memory of those who died. A young minister was conducting the service, and in the midst of the service there was an angered mourner who shouted out, "Where was God when this happened?" Those words echoed down through the Grand Canyon. This man was simply saying, "How could God allow something like this to happen?"

The young minister replied in one of the most profound manners I think I've ever heard. He responded, "God was in the same place He was when His Son died."

That story came to my mind as I stood over the bedside of my dying son. As bruised and bloody as my son appeared to be lying there, it was nothing compared to what God's only begotten Son endured on Calvary, so that you, my son, and whoever else is willing to call upon the name of the Lord, can be saved and possess eternal life. This brought comfort to me during this time, revealing to me God had a purpose in this. There would be no greater purpose than for my son's death to point to the death of God's Son.

Due to COVID restrictions, there weren't many allowed in the hospital to visit. Thankfully, the hospital allowed our immediate family to come in and see Layke. The ones who couldn't come in stayed in the parking lot to support, as family gathered inside to see Layke and to say their last goodbyes. I had never witnessed my dad so touched by something as he was in this moment. Others were very upset as well, but his reaction was very noticeable to me. There was no doubt Layke had touched the hearts of so many people, especially his own family. There was so much grace given to all those who had to say goodbye to him.

The time came when we had to let him go. They brought in a chair for Candace to sit in because she was going to hold him as Layke took his last breath. I originally thought this would be a time of uncontrollable emotions. Most definitely, this would have been, had it not been for God's grace that continuously covered us. There was such a calm in that room as we began the process of taking Layke off life support. Candace sat in the chair while I knelt beside her. The nurses then placed Layke into my wife's arms. When they handed him over to her, my mind went back to the day he was born. I thought about how they handed him to us right after his birth. I thought about photographs I had looked back on of us holding him smiling because of the new life we had just gained into our family. I thought how in that moment at his birth, we never dreamed we would be in this moment, at his death.

We sat there and loved on him and each held him for quite some time. It seemed as though it had been an eternity since we held him in our arms. We talked about him and all the wonderful memories we had of him. We agreed that even if we knew in the beginning this would be where this road would lead us, it would still be worth it just to have had this precious gift in our home. We looked at him, and he was just as beautiful that day as he had ever been. As a parent you desire to be there for your children in any battle they face. Candace and I were privileged to be there for Layke in every battle he faced in life, even the last battle, death itself. To look at his body that day, it would appear he lost his fight in this life, but that wasn't the truth. Our son Layke was victorious that day. When you think of where he was going, it cannot be viewed as a loss, but victory. He won his fight, he just did it quicker than most.

Grace in the Grip

The time came to take Layke off life support. Little did we know God was going to allow us to experience another act of grace during this time. As they turned the machine off and we watched our precious son make his way from this life to the next, we noticed his body made a few movements, but the last thing he did was something that was all too familiar to us. The first thing we ever noticed about Layke after he was born was how strong of a grip he had. We noticed this when he would grip your finger or whatever he could get a hold of. I remember bragging on Layke and his grip in the NICU right after he was born. In those fleeting moments, he squeezed Candace's hand just as he did many times before. God allowed us to experience this little reminder, and it made such a difference in that time. This let us know that God was working through it all. I remember my wife praying, "Lord, take him from my arms and place him in Yours."

After we were sure he had made the crossing, the doctor came around and listened to his heart, confirming Layke had passed. I had never been in the presence of someone as they passed away until this day. All I know is that we experienced the grace of God during that hour. The pain when the doctor told us his heart stopped was not there, and we recognized that, and the only explanation for that is God's Grace.

Grace for When He is Gone

We knew we had been surrounded by grace this whole time. However, God's grace didn't cease when Layke passed into eternity. God continued to give us grace after he was gone. Throughout Layke's life, I was amazed at the motherly love my wife showed him. This was evident through all the sacrifices she made, and the effort she put into him. However, I never witnessed this like I did the day he died. Our son's body had been through so much the past few days, due to all the lifesaving measures the doctors and nurses performed on him. It was hard to see our precious son with the blood, bruising, and all the swelling his little body had. They informed us they would give him a bath before sending him down to the morgue, and would

WHEN GOD GIVES A GIFT

make handprints and footprints for keepsakes. I remember Candace said she wanted to give him the bath. So she, I, and a few other family members gave our son his last bath.

Candace was always particular over Layke's care, but she was even more particular that day as she washed his body for the last time. She always loved fixing his hair, and of course she was going to be the one to fix it then as well. She worked for hours removing the glue that was left in his beautiful blonde hair from the electrodes that were once there to monitor his brainwave activity. We finished up his bath, making sure he was clean and just the way we wanted him. We helped the bereavement nurse gather foot and handprints for keepsakes we would cherish forever. As I look back on these events, I can't understand how we were able to do these things. The only explanation is God's Grace.

Grace for Going Home

This, for sure, was a day filled with grief, heartache, pain, and sorrow. On the flip side, this was a day filled with grace as well. For the last thing we did was something I knew we wouldn't have been able to do had it not been for God's grace. God gave us grace to go home. We had gone home many times from the hospital, but we had never gone home without Layke. Through all of his hospital stays, he never stayed one complete night by himself in the hospital. I realized Layke was no longer in his body, he was in the presence of our Lord, but still it was very hard for us to leave that night.

I remember vividly the nurse who helped take care of Layke the last day of his life. She and my wife talked, and we learned she was a pastor's daughter. Imagine that. God has people everywhere to be a help to those in need. She came to us with tear-filled eyes and told us that normally they take children who

99

had passed down to the morgue in a little red wagon, but she told us that she would personally carry our son down in her arms. This was comforting to us, as we were getting ready to leave. My wife and that nurse embraced one another and cried together. I heard my wife tell her, "Thank you, that means so much to me."

As we began walking towards the exit doors, doctors and nurses approached us and gave comforting words to us. Some even gave us cards they had written to be a help to us. We were doing something we had never done, leaving without Layke. We had his diaper bag that always accompanied him, but not him. As we walked out with our dear family, we left the hospital leaving a piece of our hearts behind.

I kept thinking, *If I can get to the next step of this process, it will get easier.* I thought that once we completed the keepsakes and the bath, then leaving would be easier. I thought once we left and got in the car it would get easier. I thought once we arrived home it would get easier. However, that wasn't the case. As a matter of fact, with each step we completed it seemed to get harder and harder. I remember thinking, *If we can just get loaded up in the car and headed toward home, the pain would ease.* However, the first thing I saw when I opened the door was Layke's car seat carrier. It was empty as it sat there in the back seat of our car. It was like reality punched me right in the gut. We traveled that one hour trip up highway 421. I thought, *If I can just get to the house it would get easier.* But as we walked through the door, the first thing we saw was Layke's highchair sitting next to the counter, just as we had left it. Then we looked in the living room and saw his exersaucer and toys sitting on the floor. It seemed that everything in the house screamed of Layke as we walked in.

There were family and close friends who came over that night to help us get settled in and ready for bed. Many offered to stay with us, but we felt it needed to be just us. As I had been thinking all evening, *If I can just make it to the next step it would hopefully get easier*, I begin saying to myself, *If I can just get to bed, it will surely be better.* Little did I know that possibly the hardest time was to come. Everyone left and we made our way back to our bedroom. When we walked in the room, there sat Layke's bassinet right next to our bed. This was the very place where he had slept his entire life, right next to my wife's side of the bed. In that bassinet was a visible stain where his head laid each and every night. We recalled waking up and looking over at him, only to see him snoozing away with his eyes half-cracked, while making a slight snoring sound. When we saw that stain outline of his sweet head, it flooded our minds with these precious memories, and we broke. I watched my wife lay over that bassinet, as she put her face right in that stain and began to weep. She did this for quite some time. As her husband, I had never felt so helpless in all my life.

We finally went to bed. Sunday night was the last night we had really slept, and it was now Wednesday night. We would doze off and naturally we would wake up and look over to the bassinet, only to find it empty, but yet it was full of reality.

After this night we would begin another step, which is described in the next chapter. The only way we made it through all of this was simply God's Grace. Apart from that, I do not know what we would have done. I can't imagine someone going through that without the grace and hope we have in Jesus Christ.

Leaving the hospital the night of Layke's death, we were left with many questions. We were aware God orchestrated each and every event according to His will, but even the medical team could not pinpoint his actual cause of death at that time. Layke's physician informed us he would be in close contact with us following the autopsy, and that hopefully we would have some more clear answers following that. It was about a month and a half before we received a call with the autopsy report. They revealed to us after gathering all the information they had, and making the most logical conclusion, that Layke suffered from something called *hemophagocytic lymphohistiocytosis*[5] (HLH). Layke's tests, signs, and symptoms revealed this was the most logical reason for Layke's death.

Our son still suffered from rhinovirus, which was what he was originally diagnosed with. As his hospital stay continued, a downward spiral of events took place. This led us and the medical team to believe something more may have been the reason for his death. HLH is a rare disease in which one's body is filled with an overactive amount of killer cells. These cells are typically present in one's body to attack harmful infections, however in HLH these cells target their own body's organs. This in turn will destroy the function of the liver, brain, bone marrow, and other organs.

Getting closure over your child's death is not something I believe comes following an autopsy report. Being given a reason for Layke's death did not make the loss of our son any easier, however we are thankful for the ability and knowledge given in order for them to make this conclusion. Oftentimes, having answers and seeing part of the why can make us as humans feel better about a situation. Although this certainly did not take away the pain we experienced after the loss of our son, we can say our Heavenly Father has not failed us yet. He has a purpose and a reason for taking our son at such a young age. Ultimately, the Lord knows the why in each and every one's circumstance. Sometimes it is not always meant for us to see. This is where complete trust in Him comes into play in our lives.

---

[5] Hemophagocytic lymphohistiocytosis, also known as haemophagocytic lymphohistiocytosis, and hemophagocytic or haemophagocytic syndrome, is an uncommon hematologic disorder seen more often in children than in adults. —Wikipedia

Chapter 9:

The Burial of This Gift

IF YOU HAVE ever had a loved one or close friend pass, you know that following their passing are arrangements that must be made. Those who have done it know there is a lot that goes into planning a funeral. You are already dealing with the pain, grief, and the shock of losing a loved one. Then there is the stress of making sure everything is just right to best honor their memory. For the entirety of Layke's life we wanted what was best for him. His funeral seemed to be the last thing we could do for him. We wanted it to be as perfect as it could be. In the process, we recognized how the Lord worked in all areas of his life, and how He graciously gave us the opportunity to care for Layke the best we could.

Candace's dad is the funeral director at Adams Funeral Home in our hometown. So of course, that was the funeral home of choice for our son. The day following Layke's death we had to meet as a family at the funeral home to make arrangements. Our immediate family, our pastor, and Candace's grandfather were all there. Many decisions had to be made, decisions far from appealing. No one wants to write out an obituary for their child. Nor is it enjoyable picking out a casket for your child. However, this is a reality that many parents have had to face, and if the Lord tarries[6] there will be many more to follow.

The funeral home had two infant caskets out on display for us to look at and potentially choose from. However, Candace and I both desired a wooden casket for him. The only problem was they didn't have any wooden caskets available for us. They began to check with surrounding casket companies they could order from, with no success. Reluctantly, we were afraid we were going to have to select one of the non-wooden caskets. As the meeting continued, the secretary came into the room and stated she had found a place in Georgia that makes infant wooden caskets. As she proceeded to call them, they informed her they would gladly make the casket that afternoon and have it shipped overnight to be there in time for the viewing. I do not look at caskets as appealing or beautiful, considering the reasoning behind why they are used. However, we were very pleased with the casket our son was laid in, and it couldn't have been more perfect. We look back on this situation, and we're so grateful for the Lord working that out for us.

I am very grateful I haven't had to deal with many deaths of those close to me, such as Layke. With little to no experience in these things, we didn't know what might be involved. After Layke passed his doctor at Wake Forest Baptist hospital asked us about doing an autopsy. Hours and even days after his death, we were

---

[6] "If the Lord tarries (common expression among Christians); just what does that mean? To most of us, it means that if the Rapture does not occur in the immediate future as we are hoping, we will take such and such an action."
—https://a-new-name.com/observations/if-the-lord-tarries/

not given a clear answer of Layke's cause of death. Everything spiraled downward so quickly moments before he passed away, it seemed as if even the doctors were at a loss for words. We were aware of several factors that led to his death, however nothing to pinpoint or give us a definite answer. Prior to his transfer to the intensive care unit his oxygen levels were plummeting. Moments after his transfer, his blood pressure continued to drop with unknown reasoning. This soon led to the critical care team needing to intubate our son. After this course of action was taken, we were regretfully informed that Layke was not responding well. Soon after, we were told his heart had suddenly stopped. Due to the madness and rapid decrease in our son's health, we wanted clear answers and the doctor asked us if we wanted to do a full autopsy. We would have answered yes to that question, had Candace's dad not been there. He is a funeral director, and he had knowledge of what a full autopsy would entail. He informed us that we did not want to do a full autopsy, if we wanted to view Layke at all. He stated that during a full autopsy they would have to look at his brain and it would disfigure his skull. We chose to do an autopsy from the neck down to determine what happened. This was one of the many ways God was looking out for us during this time, for at Layke's viewing we would be very grateful for this.

After making the arrangements on Thursday, we had to choose the outfit we would lay Layke to rest in. Due to his swelling we were afraid none of his current dress clothes would work. Candace always made sure both of our children were dressed their best wherever we were going, but she wanted to make sure he was especially dressed his best for this. This would be the last outfit we would see Layke in, in this life, and she wanted it to be special. So she and a few others went and picked out a brand new outfit for him to be buried in. We also gathered many different pictures of Layke for a DVD video to be shown during his viewing. It seemed there was a lot of pressure to get everything in order and lined up. Many of our family and friends aided in this task, for which we were so grateful.

Friday rolled around and it came time for us to go to the funeral home for his viewing. We did not have a public viewing due to COVID, just a private viewing for our families. I was very nervous about how our son was going to look. The last time we saw him, he was very swollen and bruised from all of the trauma his little body endured. I remember as we walked into the chapel where his body lay, and as we approached, we noticed there was no swelling, there was no bruising—to be honest he looked beautiful laying there.

"He looks just like an angel," she said.

To us this was an absolute miracle. I thought there was no way he could have looked that perfect after what his body endured. The embalmer was working as one of the funeral attendants that evening. Candace and I both approached him and thanked him for the wonderful job he did with our son. Tears filled our eyes, as well as his. You could see the compassion he had, as he expressed his condolences.

I realize a lot of families have scarred memories of how their loved ones looked lying in a casket. The Lord graciously spared us from having those scars. We were and are thankful for how beautiful Layke looked. It was almost as if he was more beautiful than ever before, and sent such calmness and peace over my wife and I. As we talked to the embalmer, he told us when they arrived Thursday night at the funeral home with Layke's body, when he saw him, he bowed his head and prayed, "Lord, if you have ever helped me before, I want you to help me now." Honestly, it is clearly seen that the Lord helped him with our son, because it was miraculous how different he looked compared to the day we said our last goodbyes.

I couldn't help but think as we looked at him that night, and watched those pictures on the DVD, of another funeral I once had a part in. It was for an elderly lady from our church, and she left behind a loving husband. A day or so prior to the funeral, he told me they were married on Christmas day. He went on to say that she was the most beautiful Christmas gift he had ever been given. During the funeral I read from 1 Corinthians chapter 15, where Paul is talking about the differences between the body that dies and the body that is resurrected. Paul said,

> "So also is the resurrection of the dead. It is sown in corruption; it is raised in incorruption. It is sown in dishonour; it is raised in glory: it is sown in weakness, it is raised in power: It is sown a natural body, it is raised a spiritual body."
>
> —1 Cor. 15:43-45 KJV

I recalled what that man told me at the funeral and made the statement to him, "If you thought she looked beautiful then, you just wait and see what she looks like when you see her again." Those thoughts came to my mind once more. As beautiful and peaceful as Layke looked lying there in his casket, he will look far better than we can imagine when we see him again in our eternal home.

We scheduled Layke's funeral for Saturday, November the 7th, 2020. This was a very special funeral in our minds. However, what made it special was not just the fact that it was the funeral of our baby boy, but that the presence of the Lord was manifested in that service. From the very first song, the Lord's presence was felt. This assured us everything that happened was part of His divine plan. It gave us peace that the Lord was walking with us through this trial.

Just prior to the funeral service our entire family viewed Layke once more. After the viewing, everyone went to one of the Sunday school rooms to wait until we were ready to walk in as a family. At that time Candace, Liam, and I viewed Layke for the very last time. This was a very sobering moment, knowing that this would be the last time in this life we would lay eyes on our son. Liam had yet to see him, and we wanted him to at least see his "Brudder" one final time. As we stood there weeping, we leaned Liam down and let him kiss his head as he had done many times before. Then Candace and I kissed him as well. Before we walked out to be with the rest of our family, we bowed our heads to thank God for granting this gift to our home.

We then gathered with our family, and prepared to walk in for our son's funeral. Being led by our pastor and Candace's grandfather, we walked in as they played the familiar song, "Jesus Loves Me." After being seated, they played a recording of Layke's favorite song. It was the simple chorus that Candace's grandmother sang to him after his birth while we were in the NICU:

I love little Layke, I do, I do.
I love little Layke, I do.
I love little Layke, I do, I do.
I love little Layke and Liam too.

My wife, her grandmother, and her mother had recorded themselves singing this song in harmony, in order for it to be played at Layke's funeral. After the recording played, some of Candace's family sang a song entitled, "New Grace," which was very fitting for our situation, for we knew we had been recipients of a special grace for this trial. When that song was completed, it came time for me to have my part as a preacher. There were many people after the service who confessed to me they wondered, *Why?* and *How?* I preached at my own son's funeral. The answer was very simple. I told the congregation, "I would do anything for my children, even if it was preaching their funeral." If any other parent were to ask me to have a part in their child's funeral, I would be honored to do so, so why wouldn't I be honored to have part in my own child's funeral?

I hope and pray I never have to do something like that again, but it was the least I could do for Layke. I read James 1:17, the same verse that the Lord used to encourage us, all through Layke's life. The Lord helped me in that funeral. I had just three simple thoughts in that message. They follow:

1. "The Gifts that God Gave to Layke." It was my desire to give a tribute not only to Layke, but also all those who were a blessing to him, from friends all the way to his brother Liam and his mother Candace.
2. "The Gift of God that was Layke." I wanted to emphasize the fact that Layke truly was a gift from God.
3. Lastly, "The Gifts that God Gave Us by Having Layke." I wanted to point out the lessons God allowed us to learn, just simply by having Layke in our home. Lessons about prayer, provisions, and the importance of reading the Word of God as family.

I ended my part by thanking God publicly for such a wonderful gift He gave us in Layke, and by saying that if we knew before he was ever conceived this would be how it would end, we would still want him as our child.

After my part was finished the little children's choir from our church came around and sang the well-known song, "This Little Light of Mine." Of course this was Liam's favorite song, but we knew Layke loved it as well. Back in February of 2020, just before the COVID-19 pandemic, we were in the hospital. That was our longest stay at the hospital and it was discouraging. It seemed that we weren't making any progress. However, one evening Candace was holding him in the chair there in that hospital room. He had his oxygen hooked up and she began to sing that song. In the midst of her singing it, he started trying to sing too. He couldn't speak, but he was following the pitch of her voice by cooing as she sang. It was a precious memory we have on video. Therefore, we thought that song would be very fitting at his funeral because it was special to our family as a whole.

Following the children singing, our pastor came around to deliver the final message. His message came from 2 Samuel chapter 12. It is in that chapter King David has a child die. From that passage he dealt with how David responded in faith to the death of his child. He stated in his message, "Faith always Pleas for Mercy." Truly, if God doesn't show us mercy then we are all in trouble. In the time of trials it is always right to plea for the mercy of God. He ended his message with the thought that, "Faith is Promised a Morning." This point was very impactful, for it was tied to verse 23 in that chapter. David told the servants that stood by that day,

> "Can I bring him back again? I shall go to him,
> but he shall not return to me."
> —2 Samuel 12:23b KJV

Our faith promises us a better morning. We are thankful we have this verse in the Bible. Without it there would be many mothers and fathers living in despair wondering where their deceased children are. However, because of this verse we have assurance they are in Heaven with our Lord.

The final part of the service came when our pastor's family sang a song that was just introduced to us the evening after we made arrangements. Candace and I couldn't come to agreement on what other song to have sung in the service, until our pastor's son let us hear this one. The song, "Still I Will Praise You," was as fitting as a song for that situation as I have ever heard. Even to this day when we hear it our minds immediately run to Layke. They sang with a touch from Heaven and it was the presence of the Lord that made all the difference in our son's funeral. It helped our hearts knowing God decided to attend our son's funeral.

As the funeral ended and everyone walked out of the church that day we proceeded to Bethel Baptist Church where we laid his body to rest. This was Candace's home church where she grew up. Her grandfather was the pastor there. Candace's family still attends there, however Candace and I are members at Calvary Baptist Church. The people at Bethel Baptist Church allowed us to bury our son there. Candace's ancestors were buried there, and her dad had a plot for his family there. We could not imagine the thought of just putting him in a cemetery all by himself.

So we drove to Bethel Baptist Church, following the hearse that carried our son. As we arrived, Layke was unloaded and carried by his two grandpas, two uncles, and his brother Liam was present with them as well. We followed them to the grave where Layke would be buried. Her grandfather conducted the graveside service and told us that Jesus cared for the children. He read from Mark 10:14, where Jesus said,

> "Suffer the little children to come unto me, and forbid them not: for such is the kingdom of God."
>
> —Mark 10:14 KJV

After her grandfather gave his words, there was a song and a prayer given. That was the end of the funeral.

After the graveside service was concluded we had to do something very dreadful—leave the graveyard. We walked out of the graveyard that day, and it was a very unnatural feeling. Even to this day it isn't easy leaving the graveyard. You feel like you are doing something wrong by leaving your child there, although we know he is not physically there. The only way we were able to leave that day was by the grace and mercy of God. We were walking in unmerited strength that was not our own.

Due to the church allowing us to bury him there, he is now buried near his great grandparents and great, great grandparents. This cemetery is less than a one-minute drive from our house, so it is very easy for us to go visit his grave, and we go visit on a regular basis. Nearly every Saturday and Sunday, Candace, Liam, and I spend some time at his grave. We can stand at his grave and watch the sunset over the mountains and have done so on many different visits. When we go, we always clean his grave off and make sure everything is in order. We also have a picture frame out there that Candace enjoys keeping changed out month-to-month with pictures that align with whatever month we are currently in. Candace and I talk about memories we had with him. Sometimes we just sit there in silence. There are times we will laugh about things we remember, and then there are times we just cry.

When we go to his grave and think about all the events that have taken place, it is still hard to grasp. Part of you feels like it is just a dream and it never happened. Another part of you feels the painful reality that it did happen. Then part of you feels like it happened yesterday, while another part of you feels like it has been so long. I remember when the grass started growing where we had sowed grass over his grave. I recall Candace said to me, "The grass lets us know how long it has been," for it was hard to believe Layke had been buried there long enough for a good stand of grass to be growing there.

One of the hardest things is knowing the body of your child is lying beneath—your child who you once held and loved on—and knowing you will not be afforded that opportunity again in this life. Then on the other side of the spectrum when we look at the grass, we see life coming from death. I couldn't help but think about what Jesus said,

> "Verily, verily, I say unto you, Except a corn of wheat fall into the ground and die, it abideth alone, but if it die, it bringeth forth much fruit."
> —John 12:24-25 KJV

As we stand there we often pray God will bring much good or much "fruit," from Layke's death. It is our prayer that though his life on Earth has ended, God will take his little life and touch many others. When the grass has grown upon his grave it testifies that life comes out of death, and lets me know that one day those who are dead in Christ will sprout up when the Son steps out and calls forth those who are His own. I'm so thankful the burial of Layke's body isn't the end of Layke's story.

TAYLOR & CANDACE MILLER

Chapter 10:

The Brokenness from This Gift: Grieving Times

"The Lord is nigh unto them that are of a broken heart; and saveth such as be of a contrite spirit."

—Psalms 34:18 KJV

I CAN'T EXPLAIN how grieving works and all it entails. However, I can tell you we were broken after the passing of our son. We had been very blessed our entire lives, and had never faced a time of brokenness like we did when Layke passed. We were faced with reality in many ways. Our lives were changed drastically all of the sudden. It wasn't just day-to-day changes that took place, but more like hour-to-hour, and minute-to-minute. From the time my wife got up to the time she went to bed, Layke was in the picture of everything she did, whether it was feeding him, giving him medicine, scheduling doctor's appointments, or performing therapies. All those activities were intertwined with everything she did during the day. Getting to places on time or getting ready to go to church seemed to be true struggles. It caused a lot of frustration at times. Going from having one small child in diapers to having two small children in diapers was a big change for us. It took a lot more planning and work with two rather than one.

However, the biggest adjustment we ever made as parents was going from having two children to get ready, back to just having one. Every time we went somewhere or did something we thought about those times dressing Layke to go as well, even when going to bed and waking up. There were so many immediate changes that took place when Layke passed. I told Candace days after his funeral, "This feels like we have been let off at a bus stop in a place where you had never been and left to figure out what to do next." Nothing felt right, nothing felt the same. Everywhere we looked there were reminders of the painful reality we were living. There were pictures, there were toys, there was his bassinet next to his bed, and his high chair which sat in our kitchen. Everywhere we looked, we could see reminders of Layke.

Layke's passing affected our lives physically, but it also affected our lives spiritually as well. I had a perception of what I thought this would be like. I thought that every time I would pray I would feel the presence of God in a special way, or that every time I would open the Bible, I would get a special word from God. I thought every time I would go to the House of God I would feel His touch in an overwhelming way. To my surprise that wasn't how it was. There were a lot times I would feel absolutely nothing. This affected me spiritually in a lot of ways. I am very thankful for the times the Lord does allow me to feel his spirit, but I had to find out that feelings are not what we hold on to in times of brokenness. Sometimes the worst part about a place of brokenness, is how you feel. However, there are some strongholds we can grasp hold of in times of brokenness that are secure, and can be trusted in places of brokenness.

In complete honesty, I could give you a list of all the wrong ways I responded, or of all the things that felt like hindrances during this time. However, I want to focus on what helped my family and me during this time of brokenness because what helped us may help someone else.

Recognizing What we Needed During this Time

One huge realization for me during this time was recognizing I needed help. I realized how prideful I really was after looking around at all the blessings God had given us. In days of sunshine and bliss it seems easy to get by without recognizing the things we desperately need in our lives. However, when times of brokenness come, it puts a different perspective on what is truly important in life.

We never realized how much we truly needed God's grace until we went through this trial. I have preached about it, taught about, and heard songs about it, but it wasn't until all of this that we recognized how much we had to rely on the grace of God. Concerning Paul's thorn in the flesh, Christ said,

"My grace is sufficient for thee: for my strength is made perfect in weakness."

Paul goes on to say in that same verse,

"Most gladly therefore will I rather glory in my infirmities, that the power of Christ may rest upon me."

—2 Corinthians 12:9 KJV

It is the grace of God that takes our weaknesses and turns them into strengths. I remember when we had to say goodbye to our son Layke, no doubt the hardest thing we ever had to do. In those moments we felt the amazing grace of God more than ever. It felt as if we were clothed in His grace. I saw God's grace visibly on my wife, for the same woman, who twenty-four hours earlier was on the floor in despair, was then able to talk to doctors with a clear mind and a clear understanding of what was happening. We both said to one another during that time that we knew God's grace and peace that was with us. I can't imagine someone going through a trial such as this without God's grace. However, it wasn't just in that moment we needed it. In the days and months ahead we needed it as much as we did then.

I later realized during those days and months ahead that we would have to rely on His grace just as much as we did in the hospital at his passing. I didn't grasp in the beginning how hard reality would set in on us, but it did. There were times I had to beg for God to give me grace to deal with it all. Even the smallest struggles seemed to be mountains and without the grace of God, my wife nor I would have made it through. I'm thankful God has grace specifically for you and me for the trials we face. The grace God provided for us was grace that was tailored just for what we would need. It isn't leftover grace, it is new grace for every day we live, and it is something we couldn't live without. Although I would never desire to walk through that trial again, I am thankful to know God's grace is there to see us through. If God's grace was sufficient for Paul, then it is sufficient for me, and it is sufficient for you. Thank God for His amazing grace.

During this time we had to recognize our need for God's mercy as well. It is very sobering and humbling to think about mercy, as it is very easy to get the thoughts in your head and heart during a time of brokenness, "I don't deserve this." To be honest there were times I said that to myself. I said, "My wife doesn't deserve this." If one isn't careful, that brokenness will turn to bitterness making matters much worse. However, when looking at mercy, it is God not giving us what we do deserve. I look back and think about that nurse coming into the waiting room and telling us, "We have a heartbeat." God knew that in the end Layke was going to his home in Heaven. He didn't have to give him a heartbeat back, but He did. That was God's mercy. God knew at that moment we were not ready to let go of Layke in this life. The pain and horror of that moment when the doctor came in and told us his heart had stopped was absolutely unbearable. God could have left us there, but He showed mercy to us until we were able to recognize that it was in order for us to let go and let the Lord take over his care completely. As mentioned earlier, we didn't have the grace to let him go at that moment, so God gave us mercy until He gave us the grace we needed.

Even after Layke passed we still prayed for mercy. It hasn't been an easy road to walk, but there is one prayer in the Bible that is never denied and that is a prayer for mercy. In times when it seems like it is a struggle to pray and it seems like your prayers are not being answered, mercy is a prayer that needs to be prayed. What makes God's mercy so humbling is understanding that one must admit they deserve what they are facing, and much more. Pride and arrogance dispels in the presence of God's mercy. There is no pointing the fingers in another's direction when praying for God's mercy. The only way we could pray for mercy was to admit the problems we have are deserved. We never deserved to have Layke in our home to begin with, much less did we deserve to be able to keep him for the time we were given. Praying for mercy causes us to be thankful God even allowed us to be Layke's earthly parents. That was a gift given from a merciful God. I couldn't imagine going through this trial or any part of life without the mercy of God. I love what the Psalmist said:

> "O Give thanks unto the Lord; for he is good: because his mercy endureth forever."
>
> —Psalms 118:1 KJV

Thank God for His Enduring Mercy

Walking together as a family of four, and transitioning into a family of three opened our eyes of how needful the Word of God is. The verse that is mentioned many times in this book:

> "Every good gift and every perfect gift is from above."
>
> —James 1:17a KJV

This verse was a stronghold we could depend on. Just knowing Layke was a gift given from God gave us peace and assurance when nothing else would. It helped us in the midst of discouraging doctor's appointments. It encouraged us in the midst of struggling hospital stays. It has also been a constant comfort as we faced his passing. In times of brokenness, when things have not turned out like we would have wanted or have prayed that they would, we must recognize the need for the Word of God. The Word of God gives us truth to stand on, and gives us stability to trust in. Life itself is uncertain and unstable. The only way a believer can remain stable is to stand on something that is sure.

David said,

> "The sacrifices of God are a broken spirit, A broken and a contrite heart-These, O God, You will not despise."
>
> —Psalms 51:17

David also says,

> "The Lord is nigh unto them that are of a broken heart; and saveth such as be of a contrite spirit."
>
> —Psalms 34:18

In all honesty, the only way we knew God was close to us in this time of brokenness, was because the Bible said He was. Most of the time, it felt as if He was further away than He had ever been in our lives. However, it is the Word of God that gives us the assurance that He is near in the midst of our brokenness. The Word of God is certain and dependable, and even more so when it seems that nothing else is. It is in those times of brokenness we must trust in the Word of God, and cling to His promises. In the midst of your brokenness, plant the seed of the Word of God in your life. It will grow and bring forth much fruit.

Hand in hand with recognizing the need for God's Word, there also is a great need for prayer. During this time, I found the hardest thing for me to do was pray. It was so much easier for me to sit down and read than it was to get on my knees and pray. I knew I needed it, and I knew it was essential for my family. However, there was such opposition, it seemed. I would go to pray and I felt as if I was just talking to myself, honestly speaking. I got to the point that I was so desperate to get relief in my heart that I started writing out my prayers.

I remember one of my professors in seminary encouraged our class to do this. So I started trying this, to obtain relief from all I felt inside. I realized in those moments I was taking everything I had bottled inside of me and was putting it on paper, and addressing it to God. I was able to be completely honest with the Lord, and drain everything inside of me in a letter addressed to God. I had a preconceived idea that unless I was at an altar crying out to God, I really wasn't praying. However, I found through all of this that God was hearing those prayers I was writing, just as if I was at an altar calling upon His name. It came to me one day, that David did the same thing I had done in those moments. He wrote many prayers out for us to read during difficult times of brokenness in our lives.

Two of David's recorded prayers helped me tremendously during this trial, and they were exactly what I needed. A few months after Layke died my little pickup truck kept overheating as I would drive it. I asked a friend of mine if he would help me flush the radiator because I thought it may be stopped up. This was at a time when I was at a very hard place. I felt as if my heart was full of hurt, frustration, even madness. As my friend and I were getting ready to flush the radiator of that truck, I remember sticking a bucket underneath the truck to catch all the water and antifreeze that was in the radiator. As we pulled that plug from the bottom of the radiator, I remember seeing the most filthy and cloddy water come pouring out of the bottom of that truck. As I stood there watching it, I remember thinking to myself, *I sure wish I could do this to my heart.*

It wasn't but a week later that someone texted me telling me they were praying for me. At the bottom of their text they put, "Psalms 142:1-3." That night I read those verses, and as I read verse 2 it was as if the Lord said, "This is what you need to do." That verse reads,

"I poured out my complaint before Him; I shewed before him my trouble."

—Psalms 142:2 KJV

David wrote this psalm while fleeing from Saul. He found himself in the Cave Adullam[7]. He was all by himself with nowhere to turn but to the Lord. There is something comforting about telling the Lord what you are struggling with, and telling him exactly how you feel. Many people want to vent to others and I realize there are times for that, but the greatest help we can get is when we pour our hearts out before God. When you tell it all to Him you never have to worry about Him mishandling it, taking it the wrong way, or telling it to others. He is the best source to vent to. However, if one chooses not to pour it all out to God and empty themselves of their complaints, then they may wind up in the same shape as my truck and begin overheating on the inside. If I had not flushed that radiator on that little truck, then the engine would have blown. That is the same way it is in the heart of a believer. If you don't keep your heart emptied out and clean before the Lord, then you will overheat and blow on the inside. When you tell it all to Him, He will do what He has always done. He will help His children in their time of need. Truly, He is the only one who can do anything about the situations we face.

Secondly, there was another prayer of David's that provided a lot of consolation during this time. Several more months passed and it felt like I was back in another low spot. My heart filled up with the same bitterness, and it felt like I had no escape. It seemed as if I was going to have to live in this horrible state I was in. I felt overwhelmed with all that had happened. The devastating

---

[7] The Cave of Adullam was originally a stronghold referred to in the Old Testament, near the town of Adullam, where future King David sought refuge from King Saul. The word "cave" is usually used but "fortress", which has a similar appearance in writing, is used as well. —Wikipedia

picture of my son lying there on life support was something I couldn't get away from. I became overwhelmed with guilt thinking of all the time I may have wasted. Other thoughts of worry swept over me as I wished I would've taken more advantage of the short time I had with Layke. I was mad at myself, mad at others, and it was a very low place in my life. I found myself at a place where I didn't know how to pray, and questioned whether how I felt was right or wrong. I went to work one morning and I picked up my pad and pen and began to write. I vividly remember being midway down the yellow legal pad in my prayer, and I wrote this:

> "My feelings are no longer trustworthy and they have abandoned me. I do not know how to pray, or what to pray for in this situation. Would you please help me?"

I remember as I sat there at my desk, it was as if the Lord whispered in a still small voice in my heart saying, "Why don't you pray this?"

My mind immediately thought of a phrase I had heard sung and quoted: "Lead me to the rock that is higher than I." I knew that phrase was found in the Bible somewhere, so I Googled it to find out it was in Psalms chapter 61. I pulled out my Bible and began to read it. It was a prayer from David. It read as follows,

> "Hear my cry, O God, attend unto my prayer. From the end of the earth will I cry unto thee, when my heart is overwhelmed: lead me to the rock that is higher than I."
>
> —Psalms 61:1-2 KJV

As I began to look further into this Psalm, I realized David wrote this Psalm at the lowest point of his life. His son Absalom had been killed, and his kingdom was divided. He was away from the House of God and the people of God. He felt like he was on the far end of the Earth exiled from everything and everyone he loved. Everything in his life seemed uncertain and unstable. In this situation, David prayed unto God and asked to be led to a rock that was higher than he was. The truth is, there is a Rock for the child of God. He is stable, and He is secure. He is the Rock of Ages. The Bible says,

> "There is none holy like the LORD, For there is none besides You, Nor is there any rock like our God."
>
> —1 Sam. 2:2 KJV

I'm glad we can turn to God in our lowest places. He is our strong tower when everything else is falling apart. During our times of brokenness and when it seems nothing is secure in our lives, look to the Lord in prayer. There is always help to be found in Him.

There is also a great need for the House of God during times of brokenness. Layke's funeral was held on a Saturday, so the next day would be Sunday, the day we have always devoted to church. To be honest, there was a temptation not to attend that Sunday morning. The thoughts that went through my mind were, *No one expects you to go with all you've been through.* Then I would think, *People are going to be looking at you, and it's just going to be awkward.* However, I felt in my heart the right thing to do was to be where we had always been on the Lord's Day, and that was the House of God.

We went that Sunday and it came time for the choir to assemble. Those same thoughts came through my mind again, except this time it wasn't about going to church. It was about getting up and going to the choir. I decided, I'm going to go be in the same place I normally am when the choir assembles. I leaned over to Candace, and told her, "I'm going up to the choir, but I don't expect you to go if you don't feel like it." I assumed she was staying put, so I started to the choir. As I got in my place, I looked and there walked Candace going to her place in the choir. The choir began to sing a song entitled "The Lord is My Shepherd," and in that song, the choir sings the words directly from the 23rd Psalm. The final phrases of that song states, "And I shall dwell in the house of the Lord forever and ever, forever and ever." The choir sings that phrase over and over at the end of that song.

As I was singing, trying to hold back the tears, I looked over at Candace and she had her hand lifted in the air, praising God. That was one of the most beautiful moments I think I have ever witnessed. That would have been a moment I would have never gotten to witness at our house if we had chosen to stay home that Sunday. Due to the choice we made to go to God's House, He blessed us. That is not the only instance we received help during this time, and my pastor has said many times, "At the House of God there is help, hope, healing, and every now and again there is Heaven at the House of God." Truly, they can all be found at the House of God during a time of brokenness.

Recollecting on How God Provided Throughout These Times

Another way the Lord helped us during this time of brokenness was causing us to recollect on how God provided for us throughout Layke's life and death. The Lord made it clear to us in many ways that His hand was working through it all. In seeing and recollecting all those ways, He provided us comfort that everything that happened was part of a greater plan.

The Lord provided all our financial needs during this time. He did this in several different ways. When Layke passed there were so many people who gave to us and tried to help us. Just to get an understanding of how God worked during this time, Candace and I took a big cut in our finances when Layke was born. We made the decision that the best thing for Layke and Liam was for Candace to cut back from working three-to-four days a week. Based on the boys' needs, and especially the attention that Layke required, we felt her working one day a week was the best balance. This was a major adjustment for our family. We struggled financially during this time, but we learned from experience how God meets our needs when they need to be met. Every time we needed help financially the Lord provided. We never had to ask anyone for anything. I never spoke to anyone about any financial struggle we faced, except the Lord. When you only tell Him about it, it strengthens your faith so much more after you see Him provide.

After Layke passed we had a tremendous number of people reach out to help us. Many gave to us monetarily, and we felt so undeserving of this. However, we realized the most amazing thing through all that. We calculated what Candace would have made throughout Layke's life if she would have been working full-time as before. We realized that through the graciousness of friends, family, churches, and others, that the amount of money given would have equaled out to what Candace would have made if she was working full-time. God gave back what we sacrificed financially for Candace to be home with Layke. We witnessed several instances of God giving us what we needed when we needed it, but when we realized this, it just confirmed that He had his hand in all that was going on. We definitely didn't deserve any of that, but God graciously provided. It was just another way that God assured us Layke was a gift from Him, and that where God guides, He will provide.

As we look back on how God provided for us, it wasn't just in a financial way. He placed people in our lives to help us through this difficult time. It wasn't as if they suddenly came into our lives when Layke died, but these were people who God had providentially placed in our lives long before. He provided us with a good family, a family that offered to help, gave their love, care, and support. One's family is not made up of individuals you pick and choose. The people who are in your family are those God sovereignly placed in your life. He places them there for a purpose. God makes no mistakes, which tells me God knew who we needed in our lives the most. He knew we needed them for broken times such as these.

These are the ones God knew would be best for Layke as well. As we recollect on these memories, it is evident Layke had the greatest family support he could've ever asked for. I know it has already been mentioned, but I can't help but think of all the full waiting rooms and full hospital rooms when he was admitted. The rooms weren't just filled with immediate family, but cousins, great-aunts, and the list goes on and on. Even at his death when no one was allowed in the hospital, those same people were in the parking lot showing their support for us and for Layke. It is evident that Layke's family walked with him every step of his journey. We are grateful for the family God has provided for us.

Not only did God provide for us a great physical family, but he provided us with a great spiritual family. As stated earlier, I do not believe Layke could've been placed in a better church family than Calvary Baptist Church. They supported us, and they supported Layke. They helped us financially, they prayed for us, and they genuinely displayed their love to Layke and to us. It wasn't just the pastor who showed such great love to Layke, nor was it just the faithful members, but even the little children loved Layke. Several would want to hold him, kiss him, and get pictures with him. He was surrounded with such care of a loving church, and it meant so much to look back and think about all the love Layke was shown.

However, that spiritual family God provided wasn't just Calvary Baptist Church, it included other churches and Christians who showed Layke and us love. I can't imagine having to go through this without the love and support of God's people. There were so many who would call, text, or send cards letting us know they were praying for us. Some of them were from people we didn't know. It brought to my mind that even though Layke never spoke a word this life, he spoke to so many. There is no other group of people that will help and support like Christians will. We are so grateful to be a part of the local church and a part of "the Church (the Family of God)."

Apart from family, God provided us with wonderful friends as well. Of course they stem from the spiritual family we have, but we were blessed with friends who loved us and Layke, too. These were people God had already placed in our lives before Layke was ever born. The friends God provided for us allowed us to be able to smile and laugh during the hardest times of our lives. We were able to sit around and recollect memories of our sweet Layke, and recall memories we shared. Many of these friends went out of their way to bring a meal, write an encouraging card, or send an uplifting text just to brighten our day or lighten our load. These friends went above and beyond to help us and be good to us through Layke's life, death, and even still today. Good friends are hard to come by, and when God places them in your life, it is wise not to take them for granted.

God surely has provided us with so much. There is no way I can list them all in a book, but I did want to share with you the blessing that seemed to have the greatest impact on our lives during this time of brokenness. God met our every need, whether it was financial, or whether it was just needing someone to be there. God's provisions are wonderful to recollect on in a time of brokenness.

Realizing There is a Purpose for this Time

Lastly, one of the greatest helps to us during this time of brokenness was realizing there was a purpose for this time. I'm reminded of what Charles Spurgeon stated, "God doesn't allow his children to suffer in vain." There is always a purpose for your time of brokenness. Knowing God has a purpose in every trial or valley we walk through provides help in the midst of the struggle. In the paragraphs below are some purposes we saw during our time of brokenness.

In a time of brokenness there is a great opportunity for growth in our lives. We can grow in many ways. Most certainly, broken times are an opportunity for us to grow in the faith, allowing our faith to grow stronger. In times of brokenness we must learn to lean and rely on the Lord more than we ever have. However, there is also a great opportunity for your family to grow as well. I can honestly say that the Lord has drawn Candace, Liam, and me closer than we ever have been before. There have been many nights it was just us three and the Lord. During those times the Lord knits your hearts closer together. There has been growth that would have never taken place had it not been for God giving us Layke, and unfortunately, taking him as well.

If you look at a gardener, before he plants a seed, he must first break up the soil. The reason that soil is broken is because it is essential for the growth of that seed. In times of brokenness God always desires for us to grow. I've had to pray many times that God would break up those hard and dry places in the depths of my heart, and put the seed of His Word in those places that fruit may grow from them. When I think of this, my mind goes to a book I was listening to written by an author named Frank

Turek. The book is entitled, *Stealing from God*. He gave an illustration in that book concerning a widow who had lost her husband. Mr. Turek was speaking to this woman and the woman made the statement, "I know if my husband could come back, he wouldn't." Mr. Turek assumed the woman would follow the statement up with something like, "because Heaven is so beautiful and perfect," or that, "because he was with Jesus and wouldn't want to come back." However to his surprise the woman did not say those words at all. The woman stated, "My husband wouldn't want to come back, because he would not want to rob me of the growth that has come in my life since his passing." She went on to say that, "While my husband was here, I relied heavily on him for everything, and now that he is gone I have to rely on the Lord."

This was simply profound, and so very true. In times of brokenness we learn to rely on the Lord more than we ever had. Truly, I must say through everything that has happened with Layke, I've had to realize how weak and frail spiritually I really am. I've had to pray and ask for help concerning even the smallest matters. In times of brokenness we learn how much we actually need to grow, and it is in those times we have the greatest opportunities for growth in our lives.

Not only is a broken time a *growing* time, but it also is a *glowing* time. One certainty in times of brokenness is that your life will glow or be seen in a different light than before. Christ commands,

"Let your light shine before men."
—Matthew 5:16a KJV

When we are hurting and in low places in life, people pay closer attention to our lives more than at any other time. We have the opportunity to either glow in a good way or a bad way. There were times my life would have shown in a good way, but there were also times when I felt otherwise. Regardless, people are watching. I noticed that many times those individuals who watch your life closely are the very ones broken as well. Those who would never pay any attention to you or your family will observe how you are dealing with the trial you're facing. Our actions will certainly reflect how we are glowing, whether it be in a positive or negative manner. We can see this true in the Bible with Job. Job was in a place of brokenness. It was during that time of his life he noticed the broken piece of potsherd[8]. Any other time in Job's life he would have never noticed the piece of potsherd, but because Job was broken as well, he saw the potsherd and saw value in it. For it was that piece of potsherd Job used to alleviate him of the pain he was in, using it to scratch the sore boils upon his body.

Whether we think it is fair or not, in times of brokenness there is a chance for our lives to glow for God. We can use this opportunity as a gift and shine in a positive way, or we can use it in a negative way. I can't speak for you, but I want to use my brokenness as testimony of God's grace.

In times of brokenness we are afforded so many great opportunities that give us such fulfillment and purpose. Another great purpose in brokenness is giving. Candace and I were helped during this time by being able to give. We ourselves, had been blessed to have so many give in various ways. This was such an encouragement to us, and afforded us the ability to give as well. Being able to help someone else in memory of our son gave us a sense of purpose during this time. It was a blessing to be able to give of our finances. It gave us more encouragement by being

---

[8] potsherd: (1) A fragment of broken pottery, especially one found in an archaeological excavation. (2) A piece or fragment of an earthenware pot; any broken fragment or piece of earthenware. (3) A piece or fragment of a broken pot. —The American Heritage® Dictionary of the English Language, 5th Edition

able to help someone else or donate to another cause in memory of our son.

It was wonderful to be able to give financially during this time, but more fulfilling than that was to be able to give of our faith. There was one particular moment when Layke went downhill suddenly. God put a young lady right in front of us to try to be a help to. Layke had just been placed on the ECMO machine, and we were trying to take everything in that had just happened. Moments later, a young lady with an empty car seat and diaper bag walked into the waiting room. She flopped down in a seat across the room in a very frustrated fashion. As she sat there a few minutes she saw us crying and heard us talking vaguely. I remember that young lady said, "I don't know what you guys are going through, but I just want to give you all a hug." The young lady began telling us her situation. Apparently her little boy had been abused by someone who had watched him while she was at work. She had no clue what had happened, all she knew was that her son wasn't keeping any food down and wasn't acting like himself. She brought her son to the emergency room only to find out he had trauma to his brain, and may never recover.

We never told her what we were dealing with, but we had a room full of support surrounding us. This young girl had no one. So we went over there and prayed for this young lady and her son. The next day came and we were getting ready to have to make the decision to take Layke off of life support. In walked that young lady to see Candace and me. She apparently got word from someone that Layke was getting ready to die. With tears in her eyes she thanked us for taking time for her and praying with her while we were going through what we were. We told her that the Lord loved her, and He would be the help she and her son would need. We assured her that we would be praying for them both. The fact that we simply prayed for her during that time of brokenness had more of an impact than it would have in any other time of our lives. We have failed the Lord in many ways, but I felt like we did as the Lord wanted us to do at that moment. I think about that young lady from time to time, and say a prayer for her and her son. That gave us a sense of purpose during the most broken moments of our lives. If you are searching for a purpose in your brokenness, find a way to give. Whether it is giving of your finances, your faith, or your time. It can make a tremendous impact on another's life.

The last two purposes are the most important. The ultimate purpose of any time, but especially a time of brokenness is to glorify God. That should be our purpose no matter the circumstance, but even more so in a time of brokenness. I can't help but think of Mary and Martha when Lazarus died. Lazarus got sick, and no doubt this was a broken time for this family. We all know what happens. Lazarus dies shortly after, and Jesus comes to raise him from the dead. However, Jesus made a statement that changes the entire outlook of the situation. When Jesus heard that Lazarus was sick the Bible says,

> "he said, This sickness is not unto death, but for the glory of God, that the Son of God might be glorified thereby."
>
> —John 11:4

One may say, "Well, God didn't raise my loved one," or, "God did not heal their physical body."

My reply to this would be, "Not yet."

For the Christian there is a greater hope and assurance. Paul tells us,

> "and the dead in Christ shall rise first."
> —1 Thessalonians 4:16c KJV

The hope we have in the Second Advent of Christ is that our loved one in Christ will be raised. In that time we will be able to experience the same joy Mary and Martha experienced when their brother came out of the grave. We know this because in the following verse Paul says,

> "Then we which are alive and remain shall be caught up together with them in the clouds, to meet the Lord in the air: so shall we ever be with the Lord."
>
> —1 Thessalonians 4:17 KJV

Mary and Martha were able to sit down at the table with Lazarus again. This will be a reality for the Christian as well. We will sit down at the Marriage Supper of the Lamb with our loved ones who have died before us. So even in the pain and brokenness, know that God is to be glorified through it all. I must admit there have been times during this journey I didn't glorify God, but there was a great purpose when I chose to do so. The Psalmist records,

> "And call upon me in the day of trouble: I will deliver thee, and thou shalt glorify me."
>
> —Psalms 50:15

There will be times we fail in how we respond to our brokenness, but according to the psalmist if we allow God to deliver us and bring us through our time of brokenness, then God is glorified. Truly, He is the only one who can deliver us, and it is our responsibility to let Him do it. Truly, it doesn't matter where you are in life, glorifying God is the ultimate purpose.

When God delivers and provides the help we need, may it be evidently seen in our lives that we are glorifying him.

Last, but certainly not least, during a time of brokenness is a time in which the gospel can be witnessed in our lives. One of the biggest struggles I faced during this time was understanding "Why?" I couldn't comprehend why God did not heal my son. I never asked that question audibly, but within my heart I asked it over and over again. This was a question I kept to myself. I looked back across my life and surveyed many prayers God had answered for me. There were prayers that had God not answered, our lives would've been totally different. I thank God that He did answer those. However, in the moment I would've given all those answered prayers back, in order to have this one request answered. This request was for God to spare Layke's life. I prayed many times in the waiting room and other places in the hospital, "God, if you have ever heard and answered my prayers, would You do it now?"

As we all know, that ultimately wasn't the will of God. In the days and months to come, in the confines of my prayer place, standing at my son's grave, driving down the road, I would ask God "Why?" I wasn't questioning whether God was right in what He allowed to happen. I know God always does right. I just wanted to know what the purpose was behind it all. However, I couldn't get an answer until one Sunday morning. When I was in the junior boys Sunday School class, I had two great men who taught me and a good friend of mine. I remember God did a lot of important things in my life while I was in that class. I got saved during that time, they taught us to pray during that time, and I taught Sunday School for the very first time.

Nearly twenty years after being out of that class, one of those Sunday School teachers was speaking to me about the very first time I taught Sunday School. He told me he would write the Scripture down and give it to me. About a month went by, and nothing was said. One Sunday I was walking down out of the choir, and he slipped me a piece of paper. As I reached my pew I opened it and it read, "Philippians 1:1-30, Taylor Miller, First Sunday School Lesson." So I proceeded to open my Bible and read that passage. When I found Philippians 1, I noticed that sometime had underlined one verse. The verse read:

> "But I would ye should understand, brethren, that the things which happened unto me have fallen out rather unto the furtherance of the gospel."
> —1 Philippians v.12 KJV

It was as if the Lord said, "Right there is your answer."

I couldn't help but think there was no greater purpose than for God to further the gospel of His Son through the passing of my son.

I firmly believe many of the trials and struggles we face in our life are for this very same purpose. The greatest evidence of the Gospel is to see it working in the lives of believers in troubled times. The greatest purpose in your time of brokenness is for the Gospel of the Lord Jesus Christ to be found working in our lives.

I have heard many testimonies, messages, songs, lessons, and the list goes on. However, the greatest song, testimony, message, or lesson is that which comes out of times of brokenness. Some of the greatest victories we can have in life are the ones God brings to us in our lowest places. Though it is hard to see while we are in the midst of our brokenness, we can focus on all the good God brings out during that time. It could easily be viewed as a gift in itself. It is our prayer that someone else facing a time of brokenness could read of these experiences and be helped or encouraged in some way.

Chapter 11:

The By and By
of This Gift

A MAN WHO we all know and are very acquainted with is King David. David was a man who knew the good times of life, but very sorrowful times as well. David knew what it was like to lose a child, even a very young child. According to the Scriptures, he and Bathsheba had a newborn child who became sick, and soon after passed away. His servants questioned why David ceased to fast and pray over the child when he found the child had died. In that moment David said something that must be a comfort to any parent who has lost a small child. He said,

"But now he is dead, wherefore should I fast? Can I bring him back again? I shall go to him, but he shall not return to me."

—2 Samuel 12:23 KJV

David found comfort knowing his child was in a place called Heaven. These verses were preached by our pastor at Layke's funeral. I'm thankful these words are recorded in the Bible for us to have the assurance of the permanent abode of babies and small children who pass away. My wife and I do not have to worry or wonder about where our son is, because the Word of God makes it clear. Though we mourn and grieve over his passing, we do find comfort in knowing he is in Heaven and knowing we will gather with him in the Sweet By and By[9] one day.

As discussed, on a regular basis we visit Layke's grave. We strive to keep it clean, and looking as nice as possible. As parents you have a desire to do for your children, and that desire did not disappear even after Layke passed. Keeping his grave tidy and well-kept is a small task we take pride in. There are times we go and reflect on the memories we had with him, and how terribly we still miss him. Since Layke's death, Liam has become acquainted with playing in a graveyard. He runs around and plays, pretending he is at a playground. However, taking him there has often been an adventure. Liam has a way of taking a very sad moment and putting laughter in it. There have been times we stood at Layke's grave with tears rolling down our faces, and suddenly hear someone lay down on the horn of a car, to see a sweet, little, smiling face sticking up from behind the steering wheel, waving at his mommy and daddy. Liam has done this on various occasions.

---

[9] "The Sweet By-and-By" is a Christian hymn with lyrics by S. Fillmore Bennett and music by Joseph P. Webster. It is recognizable by its chorus... — Wikipedia

There was another instance when my wife and I were standing at Layke's grave right around Valentine's Day. We had taken flowers and a balloon out there to place on Layke's grave. Our minds went back to when he was in the hospital on Valentine's Day, a year prior, and how we had taken balloons to Layke's hospital room and tied them over his bed. As we stood there pondering on those memories, we began crying, looking at the balloons and flowers we had just placed there. To our surprise, Liam walked from behind us with a bouquet of red flowers he had taken from someone else's grave to bring to Layke's grave. Immediately, our tears stopped and we began to worry about whose grave we needed to return the flowers to.

The most memorable moment was one evening as we were walking towards the grave. I held Liam in my arms and said to him, "We are going to see Brudder for a minute."

I'll never forget what he said in response: "Brudder's not here, he's in Heaben (Heaven)."

It was as if the Lord spoke to me and said, "He's not among the dead, but among the living."

The apostle Paul says,

"We are confident, I say, and willing rather to be absent from the body and to be present with the Lord."

—2 Cor. 5:8 KJV

We know our child is with the Lord in a place God has prepared for his children. If we didn't believe in a place called Heaven, we couldn't bear the thought of never seeing our child again. Heaven gives us hope in the darkest times because we know we will see our son again. We have gained much comfort in knowing where Layke is today, and who Layke is with. Here in this chapter there are a few thoughts about Heaven that have comforted us.

The Presence of the Lord in Heaven

David said,

> "in thy presence is fullness of joy; at thy right hand are pleasures for evermore."
>
> —Psalms 16:11 KJV

A great comfort we have is knowing Layke is in the presence of our Lord. One of our greatest desires as parents was to give Layke the best possible care in this life. Although we failed in many ways, that remained our goal as Layke's mother and father. As we think about where Layke is now, and who Layke is with, we do realize he is getting far greater care than what we could have provided. It is a comfort to know he is made whole in the presence of our Lord. As much as we would love for him to be here with us, we realize Layke couldn't be in a better place.

When Layke took his final breath here in this life, having the assurance that he was ushered into the presence of the Lord made all the difference. As we stood over his death bed weeping over our child, we had to come to the realization that Layke wasn't going home with us. We found comfort in knowing Layke was going to his eternal home where he would be completely healed in the presence of the Lord. What makes Heaven such a joyous and pleasurable place is the presence of the Lord there. We are eternally grateful our son is enjoying all the splendor of that land and much more, in the presence of Christ.

The People Who are in Heaven

Many have different thoughts and opinions of Heaven. There is a lot of emphasis placed on the kind of place Heaven is. No doubt it is a place of matchless beauty, in fact there is no place comparable with the beauty of Heaven. We have heard of the streets of gold and the walls of jasper. We hear tales of mansions bright and fair, and so much more. However, I believe what makes Heaven so special are the people who are there. First and foremost, Christ our Savior awaits us in glory. If He was the only one there, it would be worth it all just to be with Him. We also have our saved friends and loved ones who have gone on before us. With each passing one, it makes Heaven more and more special. Heaven surely has grown a lot sweeter just knowing we have a child there. It is interesting to hear that the longer a Christian lives in this life, the greater the longing for Heaven is. I have often wondered why that is. However, I have learned the longer we live in this life filled with sorrow and grief, the greater our desire is for the land that is fairer than day. With each saved loved one who passes away, our desire for Heaven grows stronger and stronger. I'm thankful Heaven is a place full of people we love and hold dear.

The Prayers that God Answered in Heaven

I can't count the times my wife and I stood at Layke's grave, or sat on the couch, wondering exactly what our son was doing right then in Heaven. When these thoughts run through our minds, it brings tears to our eyes, knowing he is doing all he was unable to do in this life. We know his body there is not hindered by the disabilities he was hindered with here on earth. Throughout Layke's life he was prayed for daily. Not only by Candace and me, but several others lifted him up in prayer. Our family, our church, and our friends prayed for Layke. Candace and I are blessed to have grandparents who faithfully pray as well.

I remember the day after we found out Layke would be facing many struggles in life, we informed our families. I vividly remember what Candace's grandmother said when we told her the disheartening news of his genetic results. She said, "I believe God will heal Layke." She went on to remind us of the Scripture in the Bible that says,

"with his stripes we are healed."
—Isaiah 53:5 KJV

God answered that prayer when He took Layke home to Heaven. It wasn't the way we wanted that prayer to be answered, or really how we dreamed of it being answered. However, that is the only way complete physical healing comes, when we leave this life and enter into Heaven. Those who are in Christ will be completely healed from all infirmities when they pass from this life to the next. Most importantly, the only way we can get to Heaven is through the shed blood of Christ. Nearly every night we gathered at our fireplace to pray. Our specific prayer for Layke was simply this:

"God give him legs that would walk,
a tongue that can talk,
and a mind that can think and understand."

I really did believe God was going to answer those prayers. I thought through all the hard work with his therapies and the prayers we and many others were praying, God would surely answer those prayers. You know what? He did answer those prayers. It wasn't in the form we thought He would answer them, but they were answered according to God's divine plan.

I stated during his funeral that sometime around 2:30 p.m. in the afternoon on November 4th, 2020 Layke took his first step. It wasn't on the dust of this sin-cursed world, but on streets of purest gold. It was at that same time he spoke his first words as well. He did not speak in the stammering tongue of this life, but he began speaking in a new tongue. John said,

> "And after these things I heard a great voice of much people in heaven, saying, Alleluia."
> —Revelations 19:1a KJV

Oftentimes we have wondered what he comprehended in this life. We now can rest in the fact that Layke knows much more than we do, and understands much more than our feeble minds can, here below.

God has been gracious to give us some very heart-warming reminders of the current state of our son Layke. The most vivid one personally was a winter cold night when Candace, Liam, and I rode up to Layke's grave. The snow had just started to kiss the ground. Candace and I agreed we would love to see how beautiful Layke's grave looked in the snow. Liam always seems to do his own thing while we visit Layke's grave. There were many times in Layke's life we had Liam pray his brother would be able to walk. As we were standing there looking over his tombstone, Liam walked up and said, "There's Brudder," pointing in the opposite direction of his grave.

We causally played along and said, "What's brother doing?"

Liam responded, "Walking with Jesus."

It wasn't the simple fact that Liam saw Layke that touched our hearts, but that he said he was walking. Our minds immediately went back to all those prayers that were prayed around our brick fireplace. We hadn't talked about Layke walking in heaven to Liam. We don't base our assurance of Layke being in Heaven off of what our two-year-old son saw, but it is based on the Scriptures. However, it is comforting when God gives you reassuring reminders such as these. I'm thankful God heard our prayers for our child, and we are forever grateful that one day we will see visibly those prayers answered, as we too will join him.

As our choir sings, "We'll stroll the streets together." I'm glad that as a child of God we have the reality of Heaven to look forward to in the Sweet By and By.

The Picture of Those in Heaven

The assurance we have in knowing Heaven is awaiting for the child of God gives our hearts a soothing peace in many ways. One in particular is knowing the way we saw our loved ones for the last time here on Earth will not be the way we will see them in Heaven. For some, their last view of their loved one may have been a pleasant one, but for many it wasn't. Paul makes this clear to us while writing to the Church at Corinth. He says,

> "So also is the resurrection of the dead. It is sown in corruption; it is raised in incorruption. It is sown in dishonour; it is raised in glory. It is sown in weakness; it is raised in power. It is sown a natural body, it is raised a spiritual body."
>
> —1 Corinthians 15:42-44 KJV

There have been those who saw their loved ones in a casket and the image wasn't how they wanted to remember them. For others they saw them in a nursing home or hospital bed.

However, because of the hope we have of Heaven, we can be assured the way one is buried will not be the way one will be raised. Many went to the grave with a body broken by the curse of sin. Some have been buried with a body destroyed by disease or illness. Others have been buried with bodies maimed and mangled due to a tragedy. I remember standing in that hospital room, seeing the blood, seeing my son's body swollen, seeing him bruised from CPR. I saw tubes and wires going every direction, it seemed. It was a very hard image to look upon. Thanks be to God, the next time I see my child he will not be in that kind of shape. He will have a perfect and glorified body, free from all imperfections. We are so thankful that when we see our son again, he will be whole in the presence of Jesus.

The Pathway in to Heaven

With this chapter being focused on Heaven, I believe it is necessary to tell how someone can go to Heaven. It is a very simple path. Jesus said,

> "I am the way, the truth, and the life: no man cometh unto the Father but by me."
> —John 14:6 KJV

It is simply coming to Jesus by faith. Paul said,

> "For to me, to live is Christ, and to die is gain."
> —Philippians 1:21 KJV

What Paul is saying is that for a child of God, while we live upon this Earth we are to live for Christ, but when we die there is much to gain. That gives us hope that for the Christian when death comes to us, along comes a lot of gain. The trials and sorrows of this life we will leave behind. Knowing we have so much to gain ahead of us, gives us the strength and courage to keep pressing forward for the glory of God. In Christ alone, we have much to look forward to after death. Through salvation we are given the privilege of seeing Him face-to-face and spending eternity with Him. Graciously, He has also made a way for us to spend eternity with our saved friends and loved ones as well. In Heaven we will enjoy His presence and joy forevermore. There is only one entrance into this glorious abode and Jesus stated it very clearly when He said,

> "I am the door: by me if any man enter in he shall be saved."
>
> —John 10:9a KJV

The only path to Heaven is through the saving work of Jesus Christ. I'm thankful Jesus died for me so I can look forward to a place called Heaven.

One of the fondest memories I have of Layke, is something I experienced on a regular basis. Typically, I would arrive home around 5:30 p.m. from work. Most days Liam would be in the middle of his nap at that time. Layke, on the other hand, would normally be awake. As I arrived home and opened the carport door to enter our house I could look across the room and Layke would be sitting in his exersaucer making eye contact with me nearly each and every time. It was almost as if he was patiently waiting for me to get home. I would look forward to those moments of getting home to my family and seeing him there ready to embrace him. It has been many days since his passing, and I have opened that door several times after a long workday.

I have often thought, *How wonderful it would be to see him sitting across the room making eye contact with me.*

I don't know how it will be when I get to Heaven. I most definitely want to see my Jesus, the one who died for me, but I often wonder if Layke will be looking for me to come home through Heaven's door, just as he did here on this Earth. Oh how I long to reunite with him in our heavenly home where there will be no parting or separation.

Chapter 12:

The Blessings
After This Gift

WE WERE SO blessed to have Layke as a gift in our home for fourteen months. He is truly missed each day within our home. There's not a day that goes by we don't look at pictures and think about the precious moments we had with him. Sometimes we laugh at funny things he would do. There are moments we cry, thinking about how we wish we could hold, kiss, and care for him again. Thankfully, because of the hope of Heaven we have, we will be able to hold and kiss him again. We won't have to worry about his feeding difficulties, doing therapies, and making sure he has all his medicines, because God has healed all the physical elements he had in this life. We got to experience an amazing gift for a short while down here, and God saw fit to take him to his eternal home in Heaven. We know this was the will of God, and that He has a purpose in doing so. What He does is always right. His ways are not our ways, they are much higher and wiser.

However, it is seen throughout the Bible that when God takes away He does give again. You see this very vividly in the life of Job. Job watched everything fall apart in a few short moments. Seemingly, everything Job had was taken right before his eyes—his wealth, his children, and his health. In all of that, Job recognized where it all came from, for he said,

> "The Lord gave, and the Lord hath taken away;
> Blessed be the name of the Lord."
>
> —Job 1:21, KJV

When we look around at the blessings we possess, whether it is a job or a precious baby, they are all gifts from God. They aren't things we have earned or deserved in life. Job experienced a surplus of God's gifts in his life and Job experienced having many of them taken. When we look at the big picture in Job's life we see another principle of God. God is very gracious and giving, and that is His very nature. However, God doesn't just give once and done, God gives again. We see this in Job's life. You look at all Job had taken from him, and then look at all Job had given to him again. The Bible says,

> "So the Lord blessed the latter end of Job more
> than his beginning."
>
> —Job 42:12a, KJV

The text goes on to tell us God gave Job double what he had in the beginning. I remember one day as I was driving down the highway, I was listening to David Jeremiah on the radio. He made this statement about Job concerning the death of his children. He said,

> "God only gave Job ten more children and the reason being, his first children were not lost . . . Something is only lost when you don't know where it is, and Job knew where his children were at, and would see them again."

Those words have been very helpful to me with the passing of our son Layke.

We must say we ourselves have experienced God giving again as well. As mentioned earlier in the book, we decided when we brought Layke home from the hospital that we were going to read through the Bible as a family. Looking back we really could have done a better job at that, because there were several days we missed, and we spent time in the hospital where we were not with our oldest son Liam. Therefore, we missed probably a month of reading during those times. Of course we still read individually, but we previously only read our family Bible when it was just us four together. After Layke went home to be with the Lord we decided we were going to continue reading through the Bible just the three of us because it was something we could do to remember Layke. It was also something we did that included him, so it was special to us as a family.

I remember we were at the beginning of the Book of Judges when Layke passed, and there was probably a week or more that went by that we didn't read together with all that was going on. However, we finished the Book of Judges and read through Ruth, and then began the book of 1 Samuel. We read the first few chapters, and Candace told me one night she was feeling nauseous on and off. My immediate thought was she was pregnant. The next day I went and bought several pregnancy tests from the store for her to take. The results displayed one pink line, which meant she was not pregnant. A week or so passed, and on Thursday night we read 1 Samuel Chapter 11 and went to bed. That following Friday night we were at a friend's house and we returned home really late. I went straight to bed, and Candace went straight to the bathroom. I had almost drifted off to sleep, and she came to bed shining her phone light in my face and asked me, "Do you see two pink lines?"

She had taken another pregnancy test, and when I looked closely I could see the faintest second line. The next morning I got up early and went to buy her a more expensive digital test, which would read either "pregnant" or "not pregnant." After returning home that morning when Candace woke from her sleep, I immediately made her take this new test. We read the word "pregnant" across the screen. I remember thinking to myself about what chapter in the Bible we were soon about to read as a family. It was 2 Samuel Chapter 12. This was the chapter our pastor preached from at Layke's funeral, which made it special in more ways than one. It contained the story of the death of David and Bathsheba's baby. It tells of how David responded to the death of his child and the faith he demonstrated in such a tragic event. We tried to do as David did during that time, and although we definitely came short of it, we still set our hearts to try to respond to all of this in the right way.

The chapter does not end with the death of the baby, but with the birth of a baby. It tells of the birth of Solomon and the chapter ends with this statement,

"and the Lord loved him."
—2 Samuel 12:24, KJV

The Lord knows exactly when and how to give blessings to us, and He does so in a timely manner that causes us to look upward and acknowledge Him. Had we found out we were expecting a week earlier or a week later, it would have still been wonderful, but the fact that we found out just as we were getting ready to read this particular chapter made us recognize the Lord's thumbprint on the situation.

This reminded me of the first set of parents and no doubt countless more who have walked similar paths. Adam and Eve knew what losing a child felt like. They not only buried a child, but another one was exiled. I dare say they were much more acquainted with that kind of pain than we will ever be. One man said,

> "Before the first drop of rain fell to the dust of the earth, the tears of a mother and father fell there as they stood over their son Abel's grave."

How horrible it would be if the story ended there, but God started a trend with the first parents that would be seen down through the ages. They experienced the pain of having a child taken from them. They experienced the questions and confusion this causes. However, they experienced something else as well. They experienced God giving again in their lives. For after all of this the Bible says,

> "And Adam knew his wife again; and she bare a son, and called his name Seth: For God, said she, hath appointed me another seed instead of Abel, whom Cain slew."
>
> —Genesis 4:25 KJV

If you look up what Seth's name means, it means "granted," which means "to give." Here in this story, you see God giving again. If God will give again in their story, He will give again in my story, and He will give again in your story.

Upon discovering God gave again to our family, we decided to keep this to ourselves for nearly a month. We wanted to reveal it in a way that involved our son, Layke. So what we decided to do was to take the DVD video, containing all of the selected pictures of Layke we displayed at his funeral, and reveal our pregnancy using that. We knew a man from Candace's home church who was very good with videos. He also had all the equipment needed to do it. So we gave him a copy of the DVD and he added a clip onto the end of the video that had Layke's picture, and two captions read across the screen. The first caption read,

> "I know you all miss me so much. I cannot wait until you join me in Heaven. You all loved and cared for me so well, and I couldn't have asked for better family and friends."

The second caption came across the screen and read,

> "I wanted to be the first to let you know that now it's my turn to be a big brother! I know you will love and care for my brother or sister just like you did me. I love you all, Layke Huxton."

This would be how revealed my wife's pregnancy to our family and close friends.

A few weeks later, we found we were expecting a little girl. We decided to name her *Lakely Grace Miller*, in honor of her brother Layke. The name "Grace" also seemed to be a perfect fit because an over-abundance of God's grace had been extended to us through the loss of our son, and now this new little life was given to us in the midst of such sorrow. Of course, no child could ever take the place of our son Layke, or fill that missing piece to our family. However, I am grateful that the Lord's timing is perfect, and He knows exactly what we need. As we wait for her arrival, we pray for God's touch upon her life, and that He will use her in a special way.

We are so thankful that God gives again.

Chapter 13:

Bits of this Gift

THIS CHAPTER IS solely devoted to small snippets of Layke's life that stand out to us. There are some memories that as we look back at them, bring a smile to our faces as we remember Layke. I hope these memories will bring a smile to your face as well.

Layke's Birth

It is always an amazing day when a child is born. Layke was born at Iredell Memorial Hospital on August 15th, 2019 at 3:17 in the afternoon. This was a very memorable and exciting day in our lives when God blessed us with this amazing gift. Our son Liam became a big brother for the first time, and we were now a family of four. Friends and family were also present to share in the blessing of Layke's birth.

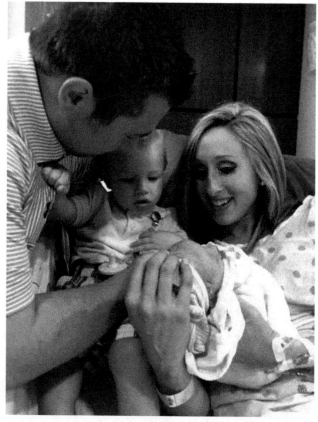

Layke's birth

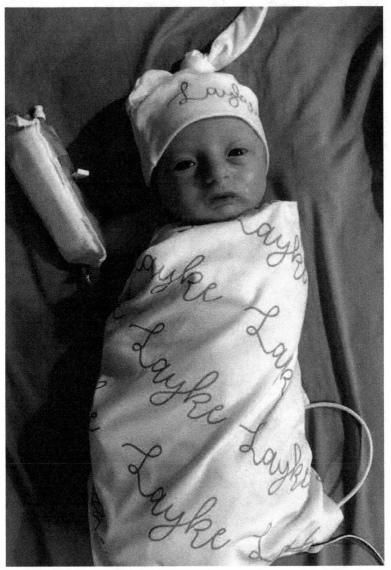

In the NICU

Family picture in the NICU

Going home with our boy from the NICU

Layke Coming Home From the Hospital

Just as the day a child is born is a special day, so is the day that you have the privilege of bringing a child home. After seven long days in NICU, we were privileged to bring Layke home where he would be loved and cared for.

August 23, 2019

Layke's Dedication

We dedicated Layke to the Lord when he was a month old. Our pastor held Layke within his Bible as he prayed over his life, asking the Lord to guide and direct it. Layke's grandparents, great-grandmothers, aunts, and uncles were present during this service at Calvary Baptist Church. This is a special memory in Layke's life that we hold dear to.

Layke's First Halloween Costume

Layke was two months old when his first Halloween rolled around. Liam wanted to dress up as the farmer, Old MacDonald. In order to coordinate their outfits for trick or treat we chose to dress Layke up as a shuck of corn.

Layke in the Christmas Play

Candace, Layke, and I were asked to be in the Christmas play at church the year Layke was born. Candace was asked to be Mary, I was asked to be Joseph, and Layke baby Jesus. This is a precious memory for us. I remember we were concerned about how Layke would do during the play. This was around the time when feeding him was difficult because of his struggle to latch. Oftentimes he would get upset due to his stomach hurting because of a milk allergy (which we later found out). However, Layke did perfectly during the Christmas play. Candace sang the song, "Sweet Baby Jesus," as she held Layke. This will be a precious memory we will never forget. (Image next page.)

Layke was selected to play Baby Jesus in the Christmas play and Candace Mary. She was holding him as she sang.

Layke's First Christmas

Layke was a little over four months old at his first Christmas. As parents, we knew this would not be a Christmas he would remember, but we still wanted to make it special. We bought him several light-up toys and played music, and also red white and black toys which were his favorite. We woke up and read the Christmas story as a family from the Bible. We opened presents at our home and later traveled to see grandparents for the day and enjoy time as a family.

Layke as a 6-Month-Old

Layke turned six months old when he was in the hospital for pneumonia. This was his longest stay in the hospital which was ten days during the middle of February. Sadly, at this time children under the age of twelve were not allowed back in the rooms since it was flu season. However, one of the nurses allowed Liam to come back into the room with us. These days are difficult to reflect upon, but the Lord was merciful unto us. If we could re-live these moments, even with our boy sick in the hospital, we most certainly would.

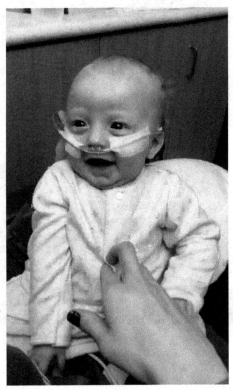

Hospital stay in February 2020

Family picture with Layke during his hospital stay

Hospital stay in Feb 2020

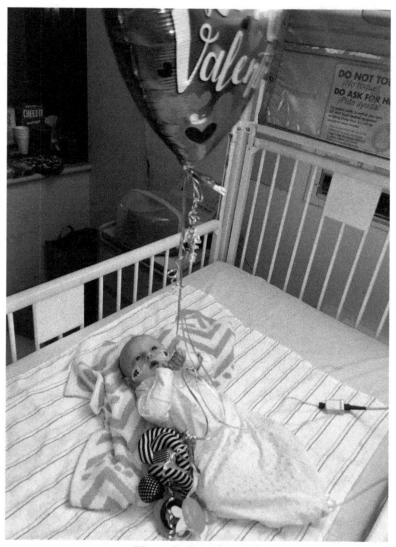

Hospital stay in Feb 2020

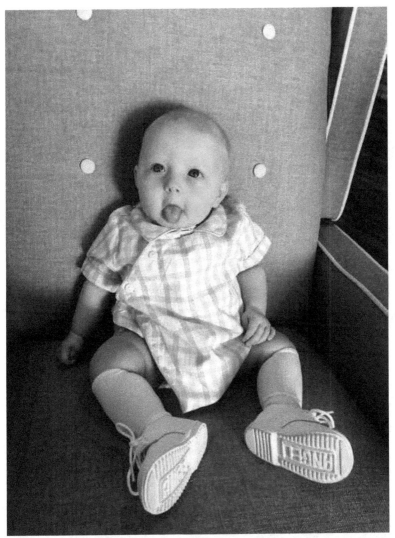

My first Easter

TAYLOR & CANDACE MILLER

Liam and Layke

Layke at the Pool

Layke spent many days during the summer at his Paw and Mimi's pool. When we took him to the pool, we had to be certain of a few things. Layke had to have a nice shady spot because he wasn't a fan of the bright sun. It seemed to irritate him, so we always made sure we found him a comfy, shady spot, whether it be under the umbrella with cushions for him to lay on, or under his shaded floatie in the pool. He usually was wearing his stylish sunglasses to keep his eyes protected. In order to make it a cool shady spot, we always had a huge box fan running right next to where Layke would lay or sit. The refreshing air from the fan blowing towards him always made him squeal and kick those chunky legs with excitement!

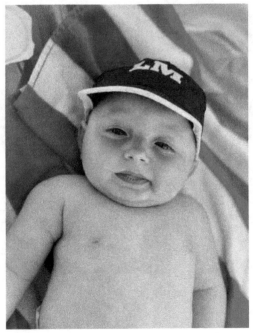

Days at the pool

More pool days

Beach days

Proud Dad

Hanging with Daddy

Layke Doing Therapies

Since we first found out about Layke's diagnosis, we were made aware he would struggle physically with his muscular strength and ability. The genetic doctor told us he may never walk and that his muscles may go from flaccid to spastic throughout his life. Regardless, as his parents, we wanted to give Layke the best opportunity in life to be as physically active as possible. Each day we would faithfully do therapy with him, striving to increase his strength.

He struggled with what would be a simple task for a normal child. He worked hard for what he accomplished. He had different types of therapists who came to work with him in our home each week. They were such a blessing and help to Layke. Many victories came for Layke, a little later than we hoped, but we were still able to celebrate his accomplishments. Some of these included holding his head up, rolling over, prop sitting, and then sitting up without assistance. Standing on his feet with assistance was also very difficult for him, as it would tire him out very quickly.

Every day Layke gave it his all to push through these milestones. He conquered many of them, but was never able to take a step, not here on *this* side. My wife and I prayed so many times, "Lord give him a tongue that will talk, feet that will walk, and a clear mind of understanding." God didn't necessarily grant those desires of our heart while Layke was here on this Earth, however, there came a day in Heaven where Layke took his first steps on streets of gold, and he uttered words he never had before. God answered that prayer, maybe not in the time or way we thought, but in His way.

Therapy time, working on prop sitting.

Talks during therapy

Therapy time

Liam Riding Layke in the Back of the Tractor

The picture of Liam pulling Layke around the yard in his tractor is a memory that always makes me smile. We never wanted to leave Layke out of anything and always wanted to involve him in what was going on. Liam received a John Deere Tractor for his birthday and it came with a trailer to pull behind. So we took Layke's therapy seat that we could strap to chairs and decided to strap it down in Liam's new trailer. We have videos of Liam pulling Layke around and Layke cruising around the backyard. Liam would often stop and turn around and look at Layke to check to make sure he was still in there. What a wonderful big brother he was to little Layke.

Swinging in the back yard

Liam Hugging Layke

There has been much said about how Liam was such a good brother to Layke. We have tons of photos of Liam hugging him. We could tell Liam to go give "Brudder" love and he would. Then there would be other times Liam would do it on his own without being asked. Liam loved Layke and enjoyed being there for him. They shared a special bond, and rightfully so as they were brothers born only fifteen months apart. Even though Liam was too young to understand it, we know that he resembled what a brother should, always showing love to his baby brother through every difficulty in life that he faced.

Layke in His Excersaucer

Layke loved to sit in his excersaucer. He would watch TV in it or play with the toy attachments that it had surrounding it. His therapist suggested this would be good for him, to start bearing some weight upon his feet in order to strengthen his leg muscles. Layke had always been behind meeting his milestones due to his genetic disorder, so anything we could do to help him meet those milestones, we would. He often sat so contently in it while he would coo from time to time.

Layke on the Lawn Mower

Something that almost every little child loves to do is ride the lawn mower. Liam still loves doing this, and I felt like Layke would love it as well. Layke took many rides around the yard on the lawn mower with Daddy.

Layke Gone Fishing

On Memorial Day in 2019 (May 27) we decided to go fishing with Candace's parents over at her cousin's pond. It was well-stocked and we knew Liam would have a good chance of catching a fish or two, so we went that afternoon. The weather was beautiful. It was sunny and there didn't appear to be a cloud in the sky. While we were fishing, Layke sat with Candace or her mom in the shade. I remember her dad got a notification on his phone that said heavy rain in the next few minutes, so we started trying to get things gathered to keep from getting rained on. Her cousin's house was a couple hundred yards away from the pond. We started getting everything together and all of the sudden the bottom fell out.

With our hands full of our belongings, the only thing we could do was stand underneath a large tree nearby. The tree kept very little water from getting on us. We were all completely drenched and all we could do was laugh at that point. So after the rain stopped we walked up to her cousin's back porch to dry out. Here are some pictures we took after we all were soaked by the rain. Fortunately, if you are a baby like Layke, you can take all of your wet clothes off and no one will think a thing about it.

Family picture after fishing and getting drenched

Layke's last Halloween. Picture taken on October 30, 2020. Layke went into the hospital the next morning and passed 5 days later on November 4, 2020.

Layke's one-year-old photo shoot

Layke at Alpha and Omega Corn Maze

One of the last things we did as a family of four was going to Alpha and Omega Corn Maze. We heard it was a fun attraction during the fall of the year, so we decided to take Liam and Layke. This was a wonderful memory for us and we got some of our favorite pictures with Layke while there. We put him down in the corn pit and let him sit and run his hands through the corn. Looking back, we know the Lord orchestrated this trip just because He knew how much we needed to make some last memories with our boy. We feel so blessed to be able to reflect on these joyous memories with our Layke. These were made less than a month from the day he went home to be with our Lord. (Image next page.)

Layke at Church

Layke didn't get to go too many places in his fourteen months here on Earth, but one place he did go very frequently was church. As we look back at pictures when he was dressed to go out, the majority of those pictures were of him before or after we went to the House of God. My wife also was able to capture some precious pictures of Liam and Layke at the last prayer meeting service Layke was here to attend. These were captured during the service while sitting on the pew. Liam was leaning over giving his brother love. These will always be dear memories to us.

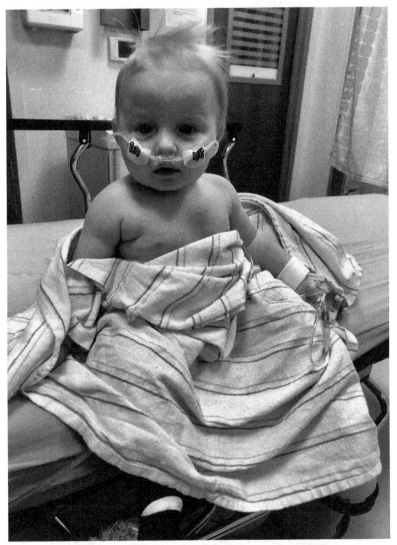

Four days before Layke passed, sitting in the E.R.

Layke Giving Liam the Piano for Christmas

The Christmas following Layke's passing was very different, to say the least. However, we wanted Liam to get something special from Layke. We decided to take the money that Layke had been given on his birthday and his first Christmas to purchase Liam his first real piano. We did this because it has been very evident in Liam's life that he has a great interest and love for the piano. On Christmas morning we read Liam a note we had written but from Layke, explaining the gift and why he was receiving it.

With Family

Sylvia and Layke (Nanaw)

Deane and Layke (Granny)

Bill & Brenda with Layke (Mamaw & Papaw Smith)

Johnny & Crystal with Layke and Liam (Paw & Mimi)

Sandra and Scotty with Layke and Liam (Nonnie & I-Paw)

The Millers with Layke

The Campbell's with Layke

Our Most Cherished Memory of Layke

Our most cherished memory of Layke would be that of his smile. When Layke smiled it made you smile. His smile was a very subtle and at the same time very strong. It could light up an entire room and it had such an impact it could change even the saddest of circumstances.

We will most certainly miss this precious smile, but we know with certainty that we will see his smiling face again.

November 26, 2019

Layke's funeral service, where the Lord met with us and gave words of comfort and peace. Although Layke was tragically taken from us we can still say to the Lord...

"Still I will praise you, still my trust in you remains." As the song "Still I will Praise You" was being sung as his funeral we worshipped in this truth.

A painting of our entire family together, which hangs in our home as a special gift.

In Memoriam

Layke Huxton Miller

August 15, 2019 - November 4, 2020

Funeral services November 7, 2020, and dedicated at Calvary Baptist
Church, Taylorsville North Carolina, November 7, 2021

Printed in the USA
CPSIA information can be obtained
at www.ICGtesting.com
LVHW011103250823
755617LV00007B/249/J